Shenandoah Valley Railroad

Through the Shenandoah Valley

Shenandoah Valley Railroad

Through the Shenandoah Valley

ISBN/EAN: 9783744759830

Printed in Europe, USA, Canada, Australia, Japan

Cover: Foto ©Andreas Hilbeck / pixelio.de

More available books at **www.hansebooks.com**

===THE===

Shenandoah Valley Railroad

OFFERS IN ADDITION TO ITS

GRAND SCENERY AND WONDERFUL ATTRACTIONS,

Unsurpassed Facilities

In the matter of Train Equipment,

And Excellent Service.

ALL PASSENGER TRAINS

On this Line carry the Latest Improved

Pullman Palace Buffet Sleeping Cars,

AND THE FOLLOWING NAMED

Norfolk, 436.

Luray, 437.

Crimora, 438.

Lithia, 439.

Otranto, 440.

Tampico, 441.

THE MOST LUXURIOUS IN THE WORLD!

Constructed especially for the

SHENANDOAH VALLEY ROUTE,

Are now in regular Service Between

New York, Philadelphia, Harrisburg, Chattanooga and Memphis,

— VIA —

Hagerstown, Luray, Grottoes, Natural Bridge and Roanoke.

QUICK TIME. STONE BALLAST, NO DUST.

Names, Location and Capacity of Springs and Summer Resorts

On Line of Shenandoah Valley Railroad,

OPENED FOR THE SEASON OF 1890.

Name of Resort.	At or Near What Station.	Distance.	Conveyance.	No. Guests Accom.	Average Board.			Proprietors, etc.
					Day.	Week.	Month.	
Antietam, Md.	Antietam, Md.	½ Mile.	Hack.	20	$1 00	$5 00	$18 00	Jos. Renner, "Renner House."
"	"	1 "	Bus.	12	1 00	4 00	15 00	Mrs. H. C. Highberger.
"	"	1 "	Hack.	25	1 25	5 00	18 00	R. F. Delauney.
"	"	1 "	Stage.	20	1 25	5 00	18 00	Mrs. John Shay.
Bear Lithia Springs, Va.	Elkton, Va.	2 "	Hack.	12	1 50	8 00	30 00	A. C. Bear.
"	"	2 "	"	50	1 50	8 00	30 00	H. A. Bear.
Fucastle Mineral Sprgs.	Troutville, Va.	5½ "	"	20	1 50	9 00	30 00	Mrs. A. Beckley.
"	"	5½ "	"	75	1 50	6 00	25 00	W. B. Hayth.
"	"	5½ "	"	15	1 50	9 00	20 00	C. T. Anderson.
Buena Vista, Va.	Buena Vista, Va.			200	2 00	8 00	Special	Hotel Buena Vista, J. W. Talley, Mgr.
Front Royal, Va.	Front Royal, Va.	1 "	"	60	2 00	8 00	Special	J M. Stinson, "Exchange."
"	"		"	60	2 00	8 00	20 00	Strickler House, J. R. Strickler.
Greenville, Va.	Greenville, Va.	1½ "	Buggies.	20	2 00	10 00	20 00	J. W. Waddy.
Hagerstown, Md	Hagerstown, Md.	200 Yds.	Bus.	150	2 50	10 00	30 00	"Htl. Hamilton." G. W. Harris.
"	"	300 "	"	150	2 50	10 00	30 00	The Bawldin, J. R. McLaughlin.
"	"	200 "	"	50	1 50	8 00	25 00	Isaac Mengel, City Hotel.
"	"	400 "	"	50	1 50	10 00	25 00	Franklin, Detrow & Fasnacht.
Hotel Laurance	Luray, Va.	¼ Mile.	"	60	Special		Special	J. Parkinson.
Arlington Hotel	"			60	Special			Arlington Hotel.
Luray Inn	"	50 Yds.		300	1 00	4 00	15 00	George K. Mullin.
Marksville, Va.	Marksville, Va.			15	Special			T. S. Brown.
Hotel Shenandoah	Shenandoah, Va.			50	Special			Shenandoah Hotel Co
Natural Bridge Hotel, Va.	Natural Bridge, Va.	2½ Miles.	Bus, etc.	400	3 00	18 00	60 00	Natural Bridge Hotel Co.
Roanoke, Va.	Roanoke, Va.				Special			H. tel Roanoke. Hotel Felix.
"	"				Special			City Hotel, Commercial Hotel.
Rockingham Springs, Va.	Elkton, Va.	5 "	Hack.	150	1 50	10 00	35 00	E. B. Hopkins, Manager.
Shen. Springs, W. Va.	Charlestown, W. Va.	¼ "	"	100	1 50	7 00	25 00	Jas. Watson, Watson House.
"	"	¼ "	"	60	2 00	8 00	27 50	J. G. Wyatt, "Carter House."
Sheperdstown, W. Va.	Sheperdstown, W. Va.	1½ "	"	35	1 00	7 00	25 00	W. S. Lemen.
The Grottoes of the Shen.	Grottoes, Va.			100	Special			Grottoes Hotel Co.
White Post, Va.	White Post, Va.	¾ "	Hack.	20	75	5 00	25 00	Miss Emma Grigsby.

I.

SHENANDOAH VALLEY—THE ANTIETAM AND THE POTOMAC.

Prue Criticises the Author.—Dutch Barns.—Ringgold's Manor.—Indian War-paths.—
Battlefield of the Antietam.—Lee's Head-quarters.—The Potomac Surprises
Us.—Shepherdstown.—Recollections of the Bucktails.—Ramsay's
Steamboat.—Pack-horse Ford and the Slaughter of
the Corn Exchange Regiment.

IT was a charmingly bright morning when we bade Hagerstown
good-bye, and took our places in the train on the Shenandoah Valley
Railway bound southward. Passengers had come in on the Western
Maryland Railway and others on the Cumberland Valley, and now
appeared after their breakfast at the station with smiling faces. Com-
parisons are odious, but a better meal than one gets at the railway
restaurant in Hagerstown is unnecessary to either health or comfort.

HAGERSTOWN STATION.

"That's a point you're forever thinking about," says Prue, a little
spitefully.

"I am, I acknowledge. It's of immense importance. Why is it I
always prefer the Santa Fe route across the plains? Because I am
sure of good meals. When one is traveling in the West or South, that
consideration is doubly worth forethought. The certainty of finding
well-cooked and abundant food was one great reason for my choosing
this route for our present trip."

"Well, I wouldn't be so particular."

"Why not? It's largely your fault if I am."

"How, pray tell?"

"Because you have educated me to so good living at home !"

That softens the critic. Prue is justly proud of her tidy and accurate housekeeping.

The face of the country roughens somewhat south of Hagerstown, and a gradual but decided change in the appearance of things is noticeable. The special feature of the German farming region is preserved everywhere, however, north of the Potomac—I mean the huge barns. While the houses are generally comfortable and some-times large, they are inconspicuous in the landscape beside the barns, which are magnificent—no simpler adjective will answer. They are not quite so big as Chicago elevators, but far more spacious than most churches. A few are built of wood upon a stone substructure which serves as a stable; but the majority are of stone with wooden sheds attached. The stone barns, having long slits of windows left for ventilation, resemble forts pierced for musketry; while a few new barns made of brick, secure the needful air by leaving holes, each the size of one brick, arranged in fantastic patterns up and down the gable ends.

The first stop out of Hagerstown is at St. James, a district full of reminiscence which Prue calls to mind at the sight of a group of buildings on the right a little beyond the station. This was " Ringgold's Manor," and Prue tells the story as we pass through the lands once under his sway.

Among the earliest settlers of this part of Maryland were the Ringgold's, whose estates amounted to 17,000 acres in one spot here, and much land elsewhere. The manor-house was at Fountain Rock, and was a splendid mansion decorated with stucco-work and carvings executed in good taste. "Many of the doors of the mansion," Prue recounts, "were of solid mahogany, and the outbuildings, appoint-ments, etc., were of the handsomest character. The architect was the distinguished Benjamin H. Latrobe, who was also one of the architects of the national capitol at Washington. It was General Ringgold's practice to drive to Washington in his coach-and-four with outriders, and to bring his political associates home with him. Among his guests were President Monroe and Henry Clay. Mrs. Clay, you know," Prue adds, "was a Hagerstown girl named Lucretia Hartt. But this lavish hospitality and great extravagance finally worked Ringgold's ruin, and when he died his estate went to his creditors."

"Yes," Baily adds, "he had a jolly-dog way of lighting cigars with bank-notes, I have read ; and each season would sell a farm to pay the expenses of the preceding congressional term."

The old manor-house was turned into St. James' College many years ago.

The streams hereabout run in deep ravines and give good water-power. At Grimes' station, the next stop, there is an old-time stone mill of huge proportions, with gambrel roof, exposed wheel and mossy flume, the whole surrounded by an orchard; near by stands the small, half-ruined stone cottage of the miller, nearly hidden in the trees, making a charming subject for a picture.

Just beyond we get a small glimpse of a river, deep and powerful, seen down through a gorge which opens and shuts again as we leap its chasm. A few quaint houses (New Industry) fill the mouth of the gorge, but before we can look twice they are gone. Such is our first sight of the Potomac.

Not far eastward of Grimes is Sharpsburg and the mouth of the Antietam, a district which seems to have been especially populous in prehistoric days, and where an extraordinary number of relics and traces of Indian residence have been found. At Martinsburg lived a great settlement of Tuscaroras, and upon the Opéquon, which empties near there, dwelt a big band of Shawnees. At the mouth of the Antietam (which flows southward parallel with the railroad and two to four miles distant) there occurred in 1735 a memorable battle between the Catawbas and Delawares, for whom the Potomac was a border line, resulting in the defeat of the Delawares.

More thrilling war history than this makes this station memorable, however, for here, on September 17th, 1862, was fought a part of the great battle of the Antietam, the more central struggle of which took place in the plain eastward of the railway. Here at Grimes, however, was the extreme left of the Confederate line, where the trees are still scarred with the bullets, and the cornfields conceal the wasted shot of that fatal day. A short distance beyond is a station called Antietam—the point of departure for Sharpsburg and its stone bridge, two miles distant, which lay at the heart of the hardest fighting. For three miles the railroad runs immediately in rear of the position held by the main command of "Stonewall" Jackson, and every acre of ground was stained by the blood of brave men. In the large brick house seen among the trees a short distance eastward of the station, General Lee had his head-quarters.

The United States soldiers' cemetery, where more than 5,000 of the Federal dead are buried, is near the village, but not in sight from the station ; from the crest of the hill it covers, a general view of the whole battle-field can be obtained.

When we come upon the Potomac again it is with startling suddenness. Out of the clover and corn fields the train hides itself in a deep cut, and thence rushes forth upon the lofty bridge which spans the noble river at Shepherdstown.

Shepherdstown lies upon the southern bank and is one of the quaintest of villages. The cliff-like banks of the river are hung with verdure, few buildings skirt the water or nestle in the ravines which extend up to the level of the town, and on the northern side of the stream the famous old Chesapeake and Ohio canal still floats its cumbersome boats. At the head of a ravine stands one of those old stone mills, most temptingly placed for sketching, and the whole presentation of the town, with the green, still river curving grandly out of view beneath it, is one long to be remembered.

Having crossed the Potomac, we are now in the northeastern

corner of West Virginia, and, in Shepherdstown, enter its oldest settlement, founded in 1734 by Thomas Shepherd, whose descendants

NATIONAL CEMETERY AT ANTIETAM.

still live there and own some of the original land.   The pioneers were
Germans from Pennsylvania chiefly, and the village has more the ap-

GEN. MCCLELLAN'S HEADQUARTERS, ANTIETAM.

pearance of a Maryland than a Virginia town.   Its settlement was
followed closely by a large incoming of Quakers, who located them.
selves at the foot of the North mountain.

GENERAL LEE'S HEADQUARTERS, ANTIETAM.

recrossed on the night of September 18, to the Virginia side, at this ford. The main body of the Confederates continued their retreat inland, but a part of Jackson's army, under A. P. Hill, remained in partial concealment, and on that bluff which you see cleared just this side of the ford, batteries were planted. This was on the 19th of September, two days after the Antietam battle. Gen. Fitz John Porter, with the Federal Fifth Corps, had been ordered by McClellan to support the cavalry, and he determined to try to capture some of Hill's guns. He posted batteries on the knolls through which the railway passes at the northern end of the bridge, and lined the top of the Maryland bank with skirmishers and sharpshooters, supporting them by two divisions. Volunteers from the 4th Michigan, 118th Pennsylvania, and 18th and 22d Massachusetts regiments plunged into the ford at dark, and succeeded in capturing five guns. A reconnoissance in force was sent across the river next morning (20th), at seven o'clock. The cavalry ordered to co-operate failed to do so, and the unsupported infantry was sharply attacked by a greatly superior Rebel force. It was driven back, pushed over the cliffs, killed, captured or forced into the river. The ford was filled with troops, for, just at that moment, the pet 'Corn Exchange' regiment of Philadelphia was crossing. Into these half-submerged, disorganized and crowding masses of men, were poured not only the murderous fire of the Rebel cannon and rifles, but volley after volley from the Federal guns behind them in trying to get the range of the Confederate batteries. The slaughter was terrific. The Potomac was reddened with blood and filled with corpses. When the routed detachment struggled back to shelter, a fourth of the Philadelphians, who had been in service only three weeks, were missing, and their comrades had suffered equally."

Thus week after week, and year after year, did Shepérdstown and the lower part of the Shenandoah valley, hear the thunders and witness the devastation of the war.

II.

THE LOWER VALLEY OF THE SHENANDOAH.

Shenandoah Junction with B. & O. R.R.—Charlestown and "John Brown's Body."
—Harewood House.—Approaching the Blue Ridge.—Berryville.—Recollections of the Early and Sheridan Campaign.—The Old Chapel.—
The Home of Lord Fairfax.—First Sight of the
Shenandoah.—Front Royal and its Fights.
—The Massanutten.

A FEW miles above Shepherdstown the track crosses (upon a bridge) the main line of the Baltimore and Ohio Railroad. The station is called Shenandoah junction, and here passengers change cars for the West and for Washington. Near this point lived a trio of officers in the Revolutionary war whose histories were sadly similar—Horatio Gates, Charles Lee and Adam Stephen. All were with Washington

CHARLESTOWN.

1. COURT HOUSE.   2. A PART OF THE TOWN FROM THE STATION.
3. HARPER'S FERRY GAP FROM THE EXECUTION FIELD.   4. OLD CARTER HOUSE.

at Braddock's defeat, and all were there wounded ; all became general officers in the Continental army ; and, finally, all three were court-martialed for misconduct on the field, and found guilty.

Before we have fully recalled these facts to each other, we cross another railway—that from Harper's Ferry to Winchester, which was so useful to Sheridan—and are at Charlestown, a place marked chiefly in my recollection as the former home of that talented and lamented humorist "Porte Crayon." The village lies off at the left of the track, behind a square mile or so of corn-fields, and is a thriving town of of about 2,500 people. It is built upon lands formerly owned by Charles Washington, a younger brother of the general, and was named after him.

Lying upon the direct course between the river-gap at Harper's Ferry (Loudon Heights rear their noble proportions just behind the town) and the principal villages of the valley, Charlestown has had its share in all the principal episodes of the history of the region. Hither came Braddock's boastful army, and a well is pointed out, close to the railway station, which was dug by them. Hither, too, was brought John Brown—"Brown of Ossawatomie"—to be hanged, and you may see a great number of relics connected with his career. The court house in which he was tried and the field where he was executed, are both visible from the cars.

This way, too, following the standard held aloft as "his soul went marching on," came the first Union troops that entered the Valley of Virginia, and every by-road, here was the scene of continual fight-ing, beginning with the "demonstration" made by Jackson immedi-ately after the battle of Winchester. Later, Sheridan and Early sparred at each other over this ground, Early having great success at first, but finally com-pelled to relinquish what he had gained.

"Why it must be near here," says Prue, as we are moving off, "that Harewood House stood."

"It stands only a mile or so toward the west, and not far away you might find the remark-able ruins of a stone church, erected during the reign of George II."

"What was 'Harewood House'?" Baily in-quires.

"A DOT OF A CABIN."

' The home of George Washington's elder brother Samuel," he is informed. "It was built under the superintendence of Washington himself, and still stands unchanged—a valuable example of the architecture of its time."

" Ah," Prue adds, " that house has seen some fine times and fine people! James Madison was married in it ; and there Louis Phillipe and his two ducal brothers, Montpensier and Beaujelaix, were entertained as became princes."

The face of the country waxes hilly as we proceed, and at Gaylord we find ourselves close to the foot of the Blue Ridge. It is no longer hazy blue, but green ; its features are distinctly visible, and here and there a dot of a cabin appears, but no large clearing anywhere. The great Dutch barns have disappeared, and the broad square faces of the Dutchmen are exchanged for the thin countenances of the Virginians. Every notch through the mountains has its name, first Yeskel, then Gregory, then Rock, then Snickers.

All along on our right, the ground was somewhat higher than where the tracks ran, yet not high enough to impede the view of the regular front of the Little North mountain, here about twelve miles directly westward. This slight elevation is called Limestone ridge. It runs lengthwise of the valley, and the rainfall upon its opposite slope drains into the Opequon (O-pe'k-on).

Eleven miles above Charlestown is Berryville, the county seat of Clarke, which has been called the "most interesting county in the valley to the student of history." The place owes its importance to the fact that it lies upon one of the great thoroughfares over the Blue Ridge—the turnpike through Snickers' gap—and to the fertile country by which it is surrounded. Prue asks why, long ago, it was called " Battletown," and I cannot tell her ; but there has been abundant reason since for such a name. Banks took possession of the place as early as '61, following the macadamized road from Harper's Ferry to Winchester. In 1864, when Early was retreating from his Maryland campaign, loaded with plunder, here occurred a sharp fight; subsequently Sheridan made this point a centre of extensive operations ; and on September 3d, 1864, by a mutual surpise, a battle was precipitated in the afternoon between a large Confederate force and the Federal Eighth Corps, which ceased only when it was too dark to see. By the way of this turnpike, too, were sent forward the great armies that pressed back Early's forces after the battles around Winchester.

A little way past Berryville, Prue calls us hastily to look down at the right upon an old cemetery crowded with headstones, and shaded by a growth of aged trees beneath which the tangled roses and untrimmed borders of redolent box have flourished unchecked. A stream, mourned over by weeping willows, creeps stealthily by ; and in the midst of the graves stands an antique chapel, approached by several roads.

"Is it not peaceful and comforting?" cries Prue. "I think one might lay a friend in such a place as that with 'sweet surcease of sorrow' far different from the bleak replusiveness of most rural cemeteries."

"Yes, and that, perhaps, is the feeling with which at a certain time every year the old families whose country seats have been in this region for many generations, assemble for a day of memorial services over their dead who are buried under those stately trees."

"I am told," Baily adds, "that its first pastor was Bishop Meade, the same who wrote a book upon the old churches and old families of Virginia, which contains the full history of this chapel."

The locality into which we are now swiftly and smoothly penetrating is one replete with landmarks and traditions of Colonial history.

VIRGINIA UPLANDS.

A mile or two beyond Boyce, for instance, we observe, off at the right, a stone house of old-fashioned style, which has been known for a century as "Saratoga," because built by Hessian prisoners captured with Burgoyne.

Then comes White Post.

"Strange name for a station," Prue remarks. "How did it arise?"

"This," I say, "was the centre of that great estate, of more than five millions of acres, granted by the English crown to Lord Fairfax, Baron of Cameron, the boundaries of which included all the region between the Rappahannock and the Potomac, marked on the west by a line drawn from the head springs of the one to that of the other river. It was the task of the youthful George Washington to survey that part of this vast estate beyond the Blue Ridge, and it was in pursuance of this duty that he made the western trips and tramped over the country in the adventurous way we have read about. Near the intersection of the roads from the two main gaps through this part of the mountains, Lord Fairfax built himself a country house of no great size or elegance ; and at the junction of the roads he set up a white oak finger-post as a guide. The original post still remains, carefully encased for preservation."

" Is the house still standing ?"

" No ; but there is a new one on its site. Fairfax called it 'Greenway Court,' and with the open, lavish hospitality characteristic of rich frontiersmen, he made it the scene of revelry and rough, hilarious sports, such as were enjoyed by the carousing, fox-hunting generation in which he lived. It was his intention to have erected a larger and more pretentious mansion, but this project was never carried out, and the proprietor lived the remainder of his days in the house first erected. Here he dwelt when his former protege, Washington, had successfully prosecuted the war for independence to the surrender of Cornwallis at Yorktown, and the deliverance of the colonies had been achieved. Strongly attached to the English cause, when told of the surrender he turned to his faithful servant and remarked : 'Take me to bed, Joe; it is time for me to die.' Old and feeble at the time, he never rallied, dying December 9, 1781."

Here Prue points out a noble height coming into view directly ahead, which seems to lie right in the centre of the valley.

" That," she is informed, " is Massanutten mountain, or The Massinetto, as it is given in early writings."

" Yes," Baily interposes, "and here, at last, is the Shenandoah, the beautiful stream that with keen poetic instinct the Children of the Forest named *The daughter of*—"

" That will do, Baily ; you don't know anything about it."

" Well, if it don't mean that, what does the name signify ?"

" Nobody seems to know, at any rate, *you* don't. Why, its very spelling is so obscure that probably we have lost the original word entirely. In the earliest accounts it was the 'Gerando,' then the 'Sherando,' or 'Sherandoah,' and the present spelling is quite recent."

" Anyhow, here's the river!"

" Yes, and isn't it a beautiful one!" Prue exclaims. " I have heard a traveler say that ' it deserves the epithet *arrowy* as well as the Rhone.' Surely, it should have a poetical name."

" And *has* a *musical* one, which is much more to the purpose," I insist. " See how graceful are its curves, how silken and green its quiet current, how deeply embowered in foliage and rocky walls, and what pretty little gateways are broken down through them to let the hill-brooks pour their contributions into its steady flood!"

A few moments later we cross on an iron bridge at Riverton, the point of confluence of its two forks—the "North" and the "South." The North Fork comes down from the other side, and its basin is distinguished as the Shenandoah valley proper, while our route lies between the Massanutten and the Blue Ridge, that is, up the South Fork. This is generally spoken of simply as South River, and its basin is called the Page Valley. At Riverton the Manassas branch of the Virginia Midland Railway (which figured so largely in army movements during the civil war) crosses *en route* from Manassas to Strasburg, and there are evidences of an important manufacture of lime. The village itself is out of sight, as also, is Front Royal, whose station is called two miles ahead. I told Baily to stop and go over there, while Prue and I went on to Luray ; and his report was so glowing I regretted we had not been with him.

To the site of Front Royal, according to Baily, came white settlers as early as 1734, and placed their houses in a sheltered nook among the hills beside the Shenandoah, at a point where the Indian trails from Manassas and Chester's gaps joined into one near the mouth of a little stream, since called Happy Creek. This fact produced a Y-shaped settlement, which, with the increasing growth of the village, has not been changed, the three main streets still following the old paths marked out by the moccasined feet of pre-historic pedestrians. Gradually the fame of the fertility and beauty of the Valley of Virginia attracted settlers from the coast and from abroad, and the Indians were replaced by hardy white men. This new settlement, then called Lehewtown, became a centre of a large district and attracted so many rough characters that it came to be known as "Helltown," with good reason. By the close of the Revolution, however, order and respectability prevailed, and in 1788 a town was incorporated, under the name of Front Royal, the origin of which term is a nut for historians to crack. From that time on it has been prosperous, having acquired wealth and fame in manufactures as well as through its rich environment of farms and vineyards. There were made the celebrated Virginia wagons of a past day, which were the best of their kind in the whole country, and were taken by emigrants to every new state and territory as forerunners of the prairie schooner. Hand-made and durable as the "deacon's one-hoss shay," their cost was so great that the machine-made wagons have surpassed them as thoroughly as the cradle has overcome the sickle ; but Front Royal still shapes and sells great quantities of spokes, hubs and other wagon material of the best quality.

Front Royal is now a neat and pretty village, of perhaps a thousand people, which is growing rapidly. As the county seat of Warren it becomes the residence of the professional men of the district, and is marked by a society of unusual intelligence.

Here occurred some exceedingly interesting incidents during the war, in one of which a mere handful of Confederate cavalry under a boyish commander dashed into the village, captured the provost guard, and made off with it successfully, though two whole regiments of bewildered Federals were at hand to protect the place. Ashby (whose birthplace and home was up in the Blue Ridge, not far away) was hovering about here much of the time, while Jackson enacted his series of victories in this district ; and on May 22, 1864, here took place one of the most disgraceful routs Union soldiers ever were ashamed of, four companies of Flournoy's Virginians attacking a thousand or so of Bank's army, entrenched on Guard hill, with such impetuosity as to scare them in utter confusion from their works, with great loss of life, stores and artillery. These disasters were requited later in the same year, however, when Sheridan, driving back Early, fought so stubbornly along this very limestone ridge which the railway track follows ; and Front Royal echoed again and again, during that and the subsequent year, to the roar of cannon, the sharper crackle of small arms and the hoofs of charging cavalry.

From Front Royal station southward to Luray the line passes through a region of wooded hills and deep ravines. The river is often close beneath the track, and its course through these rocky highlands presents many views that excite our admiration. We are fairly among the foot-hills of the Blue Ridge here, though its central peaks are far enough away to show to good advantage. In this rough district, where more wooded than cleared land is seen, a fine grade of "neutral hematite" iron ore occurs, the principal point of shipment for which is at Rileyville. A few moments after leaving that station we are at Luray, and have alighted to take a pleasant night's rest, and see the wonderful caverns.

III.

LURAY AND ITS CAVERNS.

Old Caves.—Discovery of the New Caverns.—Startling Effect of Electric Light in the Cave.—Theory of Excavation.—A Rapid Survey.—The Bridal Chamber and its "Idiots."—Varieties of Stalactite.—Richness of Color.—Musical Resonance.—The Skeleton.—A Fair World.—Value of a Good Hotel.—Luray as a Summer Residence.

PAGE valley is here several miles wide, and the surface is diversified by an endless series of knolls, ridges, and deeply imbedded streams. "The rocks throughout the whole of this region have been much displaced, having been flexed into great folds, the direction of which coincides with that of the Appalachian mountain-chain. In fact these folds are a remnant of the results of that series of movements in which the whole system primarily originated." Hidden in the woods near the top of one of these hills, about a mile east of Luray, an old cave has always been known to exist. Connected with it are traditions which reach back to the Ruffners, the earliest settlers of the valley, and it has taken their name.

In 1878, Mr. B. P. Stebbins, of Luray, conceived the project of a more complete exploration of it, with a view of making it an object of interest to tourists, and he invited the co-operation of the brothers

Andrew and William E. Campbell. These gentlemen declined to go into the old cave, but were ready to engage in a search for a new one, and went ranging over the hills, but for four weeks succeeded only in exciting the astonishment and ridicule of the neighborhood, when, returning one August day from a long tramp, the men approached home over the hill where Ruffner's cave was. In the cleared land on the northern slope, a couple of hundred yards or so from the mouth of the old cave, was a sink-hole choked with weeds, bushes, and an accumulation of sticks and loose stones, through which they fancied they felt cool currents of air sifting.

Laboriously tumbling out the bowlders, Mr. Andrew Campbell was finally able to descend by the aid of a rope into a black abyss, which was not bottomless, however, for he soon let go of the rope and left his companions on the surface to their conjectures. Becoming uneasy at his long absence, his brother also descended, and together the men walked in a lofty passage for several rods, where their progress was stopped by water. Returning, they told Mr. Stebbins what they had seen, and all agreed upon a policy of silence until the property could be bought. Then they went home and dreamed of "millions in it." Such was the discovery of the Luray cave.

Dreams are but a "baseless fabric." The property was bought of a bankrupted owner, at sheriff's sale, but upon an intimation of its underground value, one of the relatives of the original owner sued for recovery upon an irregularity in the sale, and after two years of tedious litigation, he won his suit. Previously a company of Northern men, of whom Mr. R. R. Corson, of Philadelphia, as president, had formed a joint-stock company to purchase the property, and it passed into their hands in the spring of 1881. But during the two years the original cost had swelled, while the early visions had dwindled, until they met at $40,000. This is the history of the "wonder," and now we are ready to enter it.

But it is over a mile from the hotel to the cave, and the day is warm. Enquiry develops the information that if we are willing to wait until some train arrives we may find hacks at the station which will take us the round trip for thirty-five cents ; but if we wish to go at our own convenience the clerk at the hotel will summon a hack when we please, and we must pay fifty cents fare.

I had been intending to buy Baily a certain cigarette-holder which had taken his fancy, as a present, but I reflected that, if instead I took the money it would cost, and applied it to paying the extra charge of the latter alternative we would enjoy the trip better, so I told Mr. Mullin that I would ask him to telephone for a hack at once. This was after breakfast on the morning succeeding our arrival.

"What shall I wear?" asks Prue; "I suppose it's a horrible muddy and soiling place. I shall envelop myself in my waterproof, of course, but how about a bonnet ?"

HALL OF THE GIANTS.

"No change whatever is needful," we were told. "You will find
an even temperature of about 56° Fahrenheit throughout the cave,
and all the year round. There is plenty of room to walk about everywhere without squeezing against the walls or striking your head, and
board or cement walks and stairways are provided throughout all the
area open to visitors. It is advisable, nevertheless, for ladies tò wear
rubbers, since there is enough dampness underfoot in some places to
penetrate thin-soled boots."

So Prue resumed her traveling dress—that short-skirted, close-fitting, wine-colored flannel I like so much—donned a snug turban and off we went. I told Baily he'd better leave his crutch-headed cane at home, but he his a bit of a dandy and wanted to "show it to the natives," so I had the laugh on him when it was taken from him by the keepers of the cavern, who wisely allow no dangerous implements of that kind among the fragile treasures of their underground museum.

Our road led us through the long main street of the village, but we attracted little or no attention, for nearly 20,000 tourists a year ride up and down this stony street. Half a mile beyond the town, on the slope of a low hill, stands a house with porticoes all around it and a public air. Here we registered our names, paid our admission fee, and were assigned to the charge of a guide. His first act was to hand to me a sort of scoop-shovel reflector, or sconce, in which were placed three lighted candles, and take another himself. This made us look at one another, as much as to say—"This thing is a humbug!" for we had been told of far better means of illumination than that; but meanwhile the guide had opened an inner door and invited us to follow him down a staircase of masonry, and, before we supposed our day's adventures had begun, we found ourselves in the large ante-chamber of the caverns. This unpremeditaded, unintentional entrance is as though you had been dropped into the midst of it, or had waked from a sleep there, and is most effectual in putting the stranger as *en rapport* with the spirit of the place.

The darkness was only faintly illuminated by our few candles, and I was about to remonstrate, when the click and flash or an electric arc, flooded the whole place with light. Our few candles were intended merely for peering into dark corners and helping our footsteps —the general illumination is accomplished by dozens of electric lamps hung in all parts of the wide-winding vaults and passages. As soon as I perceived this I gave my sconce to Baily, for it was a nuisance to carry it.

This first chamber is about as big as a barn (*not* a Cumberland valley barn, Prue wisely remarks), and from it we proceed upon a causeway of cement for a short distance past the Vegetable Garden, the Bear Scratches, the Theatre, the Gallery; over Muddy Lake on a planking-bridge, which is itself spanned by a stone arch; through the Fish Market and across the Elfin Ramble—a plateau in which the roof is generally within reach of the hand; and so come to Pluto's Chasm.

Gazing down over the edge of this underground ravine, Baily exclaimed: "What mighty convulsions must they have been which rent these walls asunder!"

"There, Baily, is where you show your—well, your insufficiency of knowledge! This chasm owes its configuration to the same slow and subtle agencies that produce a cañon above ground in this limestone valley."

THE HEART OF LURAY CAVERN.

"Why do you say 'limestone' valley?" Prue asks.

"Because great caves can only occur in a limestone region, since they result from the chemical fact that carbonates of lime and magnesia are soluble in water containing carbonic acid. This acid abounds in atmospheric air, and is one of the products of the decomposition of animal and vegetable waters, so that rain-water which has percolated through the soil has usually been enriched with it from both sources. Let this chemically charged water find its way into some crevice, and it only requires time and abundance of water to dissolve and hollow out Pluto's and all the other chasms, halls, galleries and avenues; and when once this work has well begun, other natural agencies contribute their aid to the enlargement of the area and the adornment of its interior.

From the chasm, where there is a Bridge of Sighs, a Balcony, a Spectre, and various other names and habitations, we re-cross the Elfin Ramble, pass successively Titania's Veil, Diana's Bath—the lady was not fastidious—and come to a very satisfactory Saracen Tent.

Then we ascend stairways past the Empress Column—easily empress of all, I think—and proceed under the Fallen Column to the spacious nave of the Cathedral. We pause to note its lofty groined roof and Gothic pillars—surely, in some like scene to this, the first architect of that style met his inspiration!—its large, Michael-Angelesque Angel's Wing, and its Organ. Then we sit down and turn to the prostrate stalactite. It is as big as a steamboat boiler, and bears an enormous pagoda of stalagmitic rock which has grown there since it fell. It thus forms a good text for a conversation, as to the age and geology of the cave, the materials for which we found by reading an excellent pamphlet on the subject published by the Smithsonian, and which may be procured at Luray. The gist of it is, that the cave is probably considerably later in its origin than the close of the carboniferous period, and not more ancient than the Mammoth or Wyandotte caves. The indications are, that in past ages the work went on with great rapidity, but that latterly change has been very slow, and at present has almost ceased.

Leaving the Cathedral, a narrow, jagged passage, we get an outlook down into a sort of devil's pantheon, full of grotesque shapes and colossal caricatures of things, animate and inanimate, casting odd and suggestive shadows in whose gloom fancy may work marvels of unworldly effect, and then are led by a stairway to a well-curtained room called the Bridal Chamber.

"Was anyone ever really married here?" asked Prue, incredulously.

"Three couples, so far, Madame," the guide informs her.

"Well!" exclaims the neat little lady. "I had no idea there were such idiots! Now if you had said three funerals, I could have found some appropriateness in it."

LURAY INN.

HOTEL LAURANCE, LURAY.

The back door of the Bridal Chamber admits to Giant's Hall, just beyond which is the Ballroom—both large and lofty apartments, constituting a separate portion of the cave, parallel with the length of Pluto's Chasm. In the Ballroom we have worked back opposite the entrance, having followed a course roughly outlined by the letter U.

I have thus run hastily over the greater part of the ground open to the public, in order to give an idea of its extent and nomenclature. To describe each figure and room separately is impossible. The best I can do is to try to give some general notion of the character of the ornamental formations of crystalline rock which render this cave without a peer in the world, perhaps, for the startling beauty and astonishing variety of its interior.

Though the simple stalactite will be circular and gradually decreasing in size, conically from its attachment to its acuminate point, yet innumerable variations may occur, as the dripping or streaming water that feeds it is diverted from its direct and moderate flowing.

Chief of all the varieties, and the one that in lavish profusion is to be seen everywhere in these caverns, is that which, by growing on the edges only, produces not a round, icicle form, but a wide and thin laminated or sheet form which is better described by its semblance to heavy cloth hanging in pointed folds and wrinkles, as a table-cover arranges itself about a corner. Where ledges and table-like surfaces —of which there are many instances in the cave—are most abundant, there the "drapery" is sure to form. In the Market it crowds the terraced walls in short, thick, whitish fringes, like so many fishes hung up by the gills. The Saracen Tent is formed by these great, flat, sharply tipped and gently curving plates, rich brown in color, depending from a square canopy so that they reach the floor, save on one side, where you may enter as through conveniently parted canvas. The Bridal Chamber is curtained from curious gaze by their massive and carelessly graceful folds; the walls of Pluto's Chasm are hung with them as in a mighty wardrobe; Diana's Bath is concealed under their protecting shelter; Titania's Veil is only a more delicate texture of the same; Cinderella Leaving the Ball becomes lost in their folds as she glides, lace-white, to her disrobing; and a Sleeping Beauty has wrapped these abundant blankets about her motionless form; while the Ballroom carries you back to the days of the Round Table, for the spacious walls are hung as with tapestries.

Do not disbelieve me when I speak of wealth of color. The range is small, to be sure, but the variation of tint shade is infinite and never out of tune. Where the growth is steady and rapid, the rock is crystal white as at the various Frozen Cascades, the Geyser and many instances of isolated stalactites. But when the steady growth ceases, the carbonic moisture of the air eats away the glistening particles of lime, and leaves behind a discolored residuum of clay-dust and iron oxides. Thus it happens that, from the niveous purity or pearly surface of the new work there runs a gentle gradation through every stage of yellowish and whitish brown to the dun of the long abandoned and dirty stalagmite, the leaden gray of the native limestone, or the inky shadow that lurks behind. It is thus that the draped and folded tapestries in the Ballroom are variegated and resplendent in a thousand hues. Moreover, various tints are often combined in the same object, particularly in the way of stripes more or less horizontal, due to the varying amount of iron, silica, or other foreign matter which the lime-water contained from time to time.

The best example of this, and, indeed, of the "drapery formation" generally, is to be found in the Wet Blanket. A large number of the pillars are probably hollow, and are formed by the crowding together of many drapery-stalactites, which finally have coalesced, leaving the pillar deeply fluted, or seamed up and down, along their connected edges. When you find one of these massive, ribbed and rugged pillars vanishing above in a host of curved stalactites, their thin and wavy selvages guiding the eye to tips which seem to sway and quiver overhead, it is hard not to believe it is an aged willow turned to stone. Indeed, the whole scene, in many parts, is strongly suggestive of a forest with tangled undergrowths, thrifty saplings, fallen logs, and crowding ranks of sturdy trees.

In more than the general effect, indeed, the ornamental incrusta-
tions of this cave mimic the vegetable growths outside. Many of the
stalactites are embroidered with small excrescences and complicated
clusters of protruding and twisted points and flakes, much like leaves,
buds, and twigs. To these have been given the scientific name of
helictites, and the grottoes of Stebbins Avenue exhibit them to the best
advantage.

Then there are the botryoids—round and oblong tubers covered
with twigs and tubercles, such as that cauliflower-like group which

A MOUNTAIN CASCADE.

gives the name to the Vegetable Garden ; these grow where there is
a continual spattering going on. A process of decomposition, dissolv-
ing out a part and leaving a spongy frame-work behind, furnishes to
many other districts quantities of plant-semblances, that you may
name and name in endless distinction. Then, in the many little hollow basins or "baths," and in the bottom of the gorges where still
water lies, so crystal clear you cannot find its surface nor estimate its
depth—where the blue electric flame opens a wonderful new cave beneath your feet in the unrecognized reflection of the fretted roof, and

where no ice is needed to cool nor cordial competent to benefit the taste of the beverage—there the hard gray rock blossoms forth into multitudes of exquisite flowers of crystallization, with petals rosy, fawn-colored and white, that apparently a breath would wilt.

But I must cease this attempt at even a suggestion of the possible variety of size and shape, mimicry and quaint device to be met with in this cavern.

That rigid stone should lend itself to so many delicate, graceful, airy shapes and attitudes, rivaling the flexible flower of the organic world, fills the mind with astonishment and bewilders the eye. And when you have struck the thin and pendent curtains, or the "pipes" of the Organ in the Cathedral, and have found that each has a rich, deep, musical resonance of varying pitch, then your admiration is complete.

STATION AND RESTAURANT AT LURAY.

The impression of it all made upon such visitors as are affected at all beyond ohs ! and ahs ! if written down, would form very curious reading ; but little has been recorded, chiefly because it is one of the most difficult things in the wide world to do adequately.

The cave has not yet much human interest ; but we must not forget to follow down a long stairway into a deep and narrow gulch, where the dampness and gloom is little relieved by anything to please the eye. At the foot of the staircase the guide drops his lantern close to a trench-like depression, through which a filmy brooklet trickles noiselessly. No need of interrogation—there is no mistaking that slender, slightly curved, brown object, lying there half out, half embedded in the rock, with its rounded and bi-lobed head, nor its grooved and broken companions. They are not fallen, small stalactites ; they are human bones. Fit for the mausoleum of emperors, what a vast vault to become the sarcophagus of one poor frame !

Out into the warm, sweet air again, all the world looks fairer for one's temporary occultation. Surely the Troglodytes had a hard lot. Even the Naiads under the water, and the Dryads, though indissoluble from growing trees, were better off!

And what a fair world it is! How prodigal of beauty are soil and sun! How grandly has the architect and landscape gardener of the globe adorned this valley! How precious the scene to him whose beloved home is here; and how novel and entertaining its features. to the stranger!

Rested and well-fed we sit upon the piazza of the inn and thank the good fortune which brought us hither. No one can appreciate a good hotel better than he whose ill-luck it was to travel in the South a dozen years ago, where that article was unknown. The people

AN "INTERIOR" IN THE INN AT LURAY.

who owned and prepared the cave, and the railwaymen who meant to profit by it, knew that the country taverns would never do. They built on this hill-top, in this midst of a populous valley which was not only pleasant to look at, and charming to ride and walk over, but which could supply all the fresh vegetables and fruit and meat so desirable upon a rural table ; a hotel constructed after that most picturesque design—the Early English—and including all the modern appliances for health and comfort. Beyond the ornamental grounds, we see puffs of steam coming from a half-hidden building. There is where the water is pumped up to the hotel, where the gas is made which illuminates all its rooms, and where the dynamo is placed which supplies the electric lights of the cave through a circuit over seven miles in length.

The *LURAY INN*, then, is not only a charming stopping-place for the casual transient tourist who stops off only half a day to see the caves, but offers an attractive residence to visitors who may choose to stay a week or a month or a whole summer. This hotel has recently been enlarged by the addition of a handsome annex containing one hundred rooms of large size and magnificently furnished, at an expense of nearly a hundred thousand dollars.

The Luray Inn is heated by steam and open fires. Elevation, 1,000 ft.; 1,500 ft. of porches; dining-room service unique and elegant. A cuisine of particular excellence; music; delightful drives. Season, from April 1st to Nov. 1st. Rates, $3.00 and $3.50 per day. Special rates by the week.

No part of the valley is more interesting. If historically disposed, the visitor may reconstruct the odd life which went on here a century and a half ago, whose quaint customs are not yet forgotten.

"Who were the settlers here at first," Prue inquires, "and what does this queer name Luray mean?"

"One question answers the other. This part of the valley was settled first by Huguenots who had escaped from France through the Palatinate ; and they named their district Lorraine, which has been corrupted into *Luray*, by changes really slight when you think of the elliptical tendency of all pronunciation in Virginia."

If recent history is more attractive, then here is the place to gather thrilling reminiscences of the long campaigns of the civil war from Jackson in '61 to Sheridan's victory in '65, which belong to every hill-top and each valley road. If one enjoys sport, here are the forests and stream of the Blue Ridge or Massanutten. If he is an artist—surely he could find no richer field. Luray itself is a relic of the old-time Virginia rural villages—quaint, irregular, vine-grown and full of romantic suggestion. Along the river, pictures of the most enchanting character may be found ; with the water in the foreground, a rocky wall right or left, a middle distance of farm lands and well-rounded copses, the vista will always lead straight to the clustered peaks that stand proud and shapely on the horizon.

IV.

UP THE SOUTH FORK.

The Hawksbill.—Shields' Pursuit of Jackson.—"Stonewall's" Personal Fighting.—Elk-ton.—The Battle of Port Republic.—Iron Mining and Manufacture.—Other Minerals.—The Grottoes of the Shenandoah.—The Way to the White Sulphur Springs.—Jubal Early's Defeat at Waynesboro.

FROM Luray southward the road runs upon a ridge separating the Shenandoah from the Hawksbill, which was crossed just at town, and whose broad valley is filled with prosperous farms. It was a favorite resort for cavalrymen during the late war, since they not only found it a capital region to operate in, but plentifully stored with forage. Through the many passes in this part of the Blue Ridge would descend the troopers of Mosby, and to the same fastnesses fled the horsemen of Early's hard-pressed squadron, only to reappear again the moment the coast was clear.

Up this South Fork, 1862, Shields hastened forward after Jackson, who had escaped between him and Fremont at Strasburg, while the latter commander chased him up the North Fork. The plan was to unite at the southern end of the Massanutten, and there defeat the weary and weakened Rebels by means of their combined forces—a plan which promised success, but failed to keep its promise.

Shields' first care was the bridges, of which three spanned the Shenandoah betwen Luray and Port Republic. One of these was just here opposite Marksville station (a place now noteworthy for the superior ochre which is mined in this vicinity), but he was too late, for Jackson had burned it. Thus compelled to take muddy roads (this was the first week of June), he struggled slowly along the western bank of the river until his advance had arrived at Conrad's Store, where was the next bridge, and which is only a mile or two from our station, Elkton, on Elk Run. (It was by the way of Swift Run gap and down this little side valley, that Spottswood and his "Knights of the Golden Horseshoe" first looked upon the Shenandoah, in 1716, whence sprang the Scotch-Irish ancestors of the land-holders of this region.) Carroll, one of Shields' subordinates, pushing north to secure the bridge at Conrad's, with Tyler's brigade, a few miles behind, surprised the whole of Jackson's trains and camp, left under the guard of only a few cavalrymen with three guns. Dashing in, Carroll nearly stampeded the train and escort, but it happened that the commander and his staff were there, and taking part himself in the very front of the skirmish, Jackson succeeded in recapturing the bridge, beating back the bold Federal squad, and recovering his equipage. Meanwhile the battle of Cross Keys, a few miles to westward had begun, Ewell's Confederates facing Fremont and holding him in check until night allowed the vanquished Federals to retreat.

All this time our merry train has been carrying us southward, and when the whistle sounds for Port Republic—the next station above Elkton—we are running straight across the river-plain on

which was fought the frightful battle of June 10th, 1862, where the
dead lay so thickly that Jackson thought they must outnumber the
living.

Here is the head of the South Fork of the Shenandoah, and the
town takes its name from the fact that formerly flat-boat navigation
began at this "port." About four miles southwest, the North and
Middle Rivers, the principal tributaries that go to make the main
Shenandoah, unite, and at this point, South River, coming from the
base of the Blue Ridge, joins them. In the angle between South and
Middle Rivers lies the town, and through it goes the valley turnpike
on its way to the crossing of the Blue Ridge at Brown's Gap. From
the cultivated river-plain a succession of terraces arise to the wooded
spurs of the mountains.

On the morning of the 10th of June, the Union army under Shields
had been planted below the town in a very advantageous position,
Jackson's men were divided, but withdrawing Ewell's army from its
position at Cross Keys, Jackson soon outnumbered the force of
Shields, who could expect no help from Fremont. The fighting began
early in the day, and was especially severe in the elevated woods
upon the left of the line of battle, where Tyler's Federal guns were
captured and re-captured by hand-to-hand conflicts in the thickets.
At first the Confederates got the worst of it, and their general trembled
for the result; but his arrangements were so careful, his celerity in
re-inforcing was so great and his men were so recklessly courageous,
that they bloodily snatched victory from defeat and pressed the
Federals so heavily that for a short time the retreat became a rout.
The loss was terrific—a far larger percentage than is usual in battles;
and though the cavalry began to follow the fleeing foe, they were
speedily recalled; and before night the whole Confederate army was
hastily withdrawing into the security of Brown's Gap, Fremont, who
had come to the bluffs on the western bank of the river, giving them
a parting salvo.

Meanwhile, Shields (and later, Fremont), under orders from
McDowell, continued to retreat to the base of operations in the lower
valley. These battles of Cross Keys and Port Republic closed Jackson's momentous and brilliant campaigns of 1862—closed them in the
very region where they were begun with a small and dispirited army
only three months before. The succeeding week he spread his camps
in the park-like groves and dells which lie a little south of Port Republic—the very hills through which the track now winds so ingeni-
ously.

But Baily, who has a practical turn of mind far above me, has been
listening to only a portion of my war stories, having gone off to chat
with a gentleman who he somehow discovered was informed about
iron matters in these hills. Reporting this conversation, Baily tells us
that this region is full of metallic wealth and has long furnished iron
and various other useful minerals to commerce, rivaling the mining

districts of the Appalachian ranges north of the great valley. On the Massanutten outcrops of iron ores, classified as Clinton Nos. III. and V., occur in nearly every peak, while universally, almost, at the western base of the Blue Ridge, primordial iron comes to the surface.

"We have just passed," says Baily, "at Shenandoah, between Luray and Elkton, the large Shenandoah Iron Works, where for many years charcoal-iron has been made, but now blast furnaces have been erected, and coke-iron is made. They tell me that the company owns 35,000 acres of land along the foot of the mountains, only a small portion of which is under cultivation, and that the iron ore is quarried out of open excavations. This place was formerly called Milnes, and is now being rapidly developed by large capitalists."

" The ore is a brown hematite, and the product is a neutral iron of especial value for foundry use. Only pig is cast now, but blooms can be made when the market justifies it. About three hundred and fifty men are employed."

" Is that all there is at the station?" I ask.

" No, it is the end of a division of the railway—you noticed that we changed locomotives; and there are some repair-shops. The result is a busy little town which furnishes the neighboring farmers so steady a market for their beef, poultry, garden produce and forage, that they are well off and enhancing the value of their lands by steady improvements and a higher style of agriculture. Sixty or seventy dollars an acre is asked for the best farms in that neighborhood, though a great deal of unimproved land may be bought for ten dollars an acre."

Iron, however, is not the whole mineral wealth of this region. Umber, ochre, copper, manganese, marble, kaolin, fire-clay and various other useful metals and earths are known to lie adjacent to the line of railway we are following, and are rapidly being availed of by capitalists.

At Grottoes station of the Shenandoah Valley Railway, on the line of the two large and rich counties of Augusta and Rockingham, 130 miles from Hagerstown, 110 miles from Roanoke and 40 miles south from Luray, is The Grottoes Hotel, a new establishment, well furnished, lighted throughout by electric lights, and kept in the very best manner by Mr. A. D. Wright, of the Midland Junction, Charlottesville, and the Danville, Va., hotels known by his name.

The Grottoes Hotel is one of the meal stations of the Shenandoah Valley Railroad ; it is also, and more especially, the stopping and resting place for visitors to the two famous caverns known as Weyer's Cave and the Fountains Cave, together called the "Grottoes of the Shenandoah," which with their numerous halls and chambers of great extent occupy the largest part of the interior of the curiously formed and commanding ridge that rises so boldly just to the westward of Grottoes station and hotel, and but a short distance away across the stream-valley of the South River of the Shenandoah and near the margin of that loveliest of rivers.

34

SHENANDOAH IRON WORKS.

GROTTOES STATION.

From the broad verandas of the hotel, grand landscapes stretch away in all directions. To the east and south, over the tops of acres of forest of pines, oaks and scores of other trees, part of the great park of hundreds of acres of valley and stream, and forests, and ridge and table-land, pertaining to the Grottoes, appear the domes, spurs and majestic outlines of the Blue Ridge. To the northeast rolls away, in graceful and varied undulations, the famous valley of the Shenandoah, five and twenty miles in breadth, from the Blue Ridge on the east to the Great North or Shenandoah Mountains on the west, a glorious table-land, from 1,000 to 1,500 feet above tide, until miles away the remarkable Massanutten ranges (Stonewall Jackson's strategic mountains) rise grandly, as a central axis in the valley, dividing it into eastern and western valleys, and the three giant mountain chains, with crest-lines from 2,500 to over 4,000 feet above the sea level, and the two included valleys stretch away until lost in the far distance.

A noble avenue, a hundred and fifty feet wide, with walk ways, carriage ways and a wide riding way leads from the hotel to the westward, about half a mile, crossing South River of Shenandoah by a fine new suspension foot bridge, from which a lovely river landscape is seen, to the foot of Grottoes Ridge, whence nicely graded walks ascend the side of the Ridge ; one to the right to Weyer's Cave and the other one to the left to Fountains Cave. From these shaded ways, canopied by a great variety of trees and vines, and bordered by rocks and slopes, rich with ferns and wild flowers, lovely landscapes embracing rivers, plains, mountains and forests, farms and villages, and famous battle-fields open and expand until the resting houses at the entrances of the caves are reached, where easy seats invite to a leisurely enjoyment of a wide and wonderful prospect.

If the way is followed that leads beyond the Fountains Cave there will be found on the top of Grottoes Ridge a plateau and park of remarkable beauty, ample groves, and plantations of pines and cedars, of oaks and walnuts, of elms and ashes, and of scores of others of the many noble forest trees of Virginia, rich flora, all so disposed as to produce the finest effects of the landscape gardener, with unlimited opportunities at his command, while from every opening a grand panorama of wide valleys and grand mountain chains extend around with a sweep of more than a hundred miles. Ten thousand people

THE CATARACT—GROTTOES OF THE SHENANDOAH.

would find room for the largest liberty of enjoyment with out-door nature in the groves, on the shaded river banks, on the grassy plains, and in the boating, bathing and fishing, all within the domain of the Grottoes of the Shenandoah. Its camping and drilling grounds are big enough for tens of thousands.

The greatest of the attractions of this place, though, are its wonderful caves. Weyer's Cave has more than a mile of halls, chambers and passages, all magnificently and wonderfully adorned by stalactites and stalagmites of all sizes, from that of a straw to that of a great tower, and of almost every conceivable form. For ages the work of decorating the miles upon miles of walls, galleries, alcoves, arches and ceilings of the scores of rooms of this magnificent subterranean temple has gone on unceasingly, with no moment of respite, with myriad handed and all knowing nature for the artist, and so no wonder that nothing known can surpass the wonderful works here to be seen. Electric light having the power of many thousands of candles, operating by the alternating system, has, with remarkable skill and at great expense, been introduced into every part of this wonderful cavern, revealing thousands of forms of stalactitic beauty, especially in the lofty ceilings of the great cathedral-like halls, from 60 to 90 feet high, that were never seen before. The noble "Washington Hall," over 240 feet long and 60 feet to the ceiling ; the magnificent "Solomon's Temple," undoubtedly the most gorgeous single natural grotto in the world ; the grand "Tower of Babel," a mighty colonnaded stalagmite over 50 feet in circumference; the superb "Bridal Veil ;" the glittering "Diamond Waterfall ;" the "Garden of Eden," a museum of bewildering wonders. These and hundreds of other objects of unfailing interest are all made gloriously visible by the admirable electric lights.

No expense has been spared to make every portion of this cave easy of access ; its floors are all dry and either solid stone or earth ; all narrow ways have been widened and steep ones been made easy, so there is nothing to hinder the fullest enjoyment of the wonders of this famous cavern. Its dry and even tempered atmosphere (always about 53°) invites to exhilarating exercise so that no one suffers from weariness or fatigue during the one to two hours generally consumed in going through this cave.

In *Harper's New Monthly Magazine* for December, 1854, the 55th number of that now widely read and almost venerable periodical, appeared the first of a series of articles entitled, "Virginia Illustrated—Adventures of Porte Crayon and his Cousins," in which was included an illustrated description of the Weyer's Cave of the Grottoes of the Shenandoah.

" Porte Crayon " was the *nom de plume* of Gen. David H. Strother, an artistic gentleman residing at Berkeley Springs, Va., at the time he wrote " Virginia Illustrated," which entitles him to recognition as one of the first of the Americans who have made its monthly magazines famous for their illustrated articles.

" Porte Crayon " spent many hours in the Weyer Cave sketching and studying, with the eye and the fancy of an artist, some of the wonderful scenes of this most varied and famous of all known caverns.—The lapse of thirty-five years of nature's never ending work in the ornamentation of her grottoes has but added to the charms and brilliancy of the scenes sketched by this faithful artist.

The only noticeable changes by the hand of man are those that have made all portions of this extensive and enchanting grotto easily accessible, and that have introduced, with skillful but conceded art, amid all its marvelous beauties, hundreds of the most brilliant electric lights that not only reveal more clearly what "Porte Crayon" saw and described, but thousands of wondrous forms of beauty in lofty fretted roofs and richly ornamented lady-chapels, that could not be seen by the dim lights at his disposal."

By the way," Baily remarks, as the train pulls up at Waynesboro junction, a mile from the large and well-known town of Waynesboro, " Hotchkiss says this place deserves a name of its own, because it is going to be a great town some day."

" Why does he think so ? "

" On account of the ease of transportation to it from four directions of the crude materials ; of minerals and timber property abounding in the region to which it forms the centre, and of the machinery necessary to their manufacture."

Just now Waynesboro is merely the crossing of our road by the Chesapeake and Ohio. A number passengers disembarked who were bound for the White Sulphur and other springs across the mountains to the westward, while some were going the other way to winemaking Charlottesville or to Richmond. To the White Sulphur and other famous Virginian mountain resorts we found this was coming to be a favorite route from both north and south, its own loveliness, the opportunity of thus seeing one or both of the two great " natural curiosities" of the Alleghanian region, Luray Caverns and the Natural Bridge, and the exceeding wildness of the scenery along the mountain division of the Chesapeake and Ohio (or of the Richmond and Alleghany for those who choose to go *via* Loch Laird and Clifton Forge), recommending it above other routes. The Madame was very anxious to go over to the White Sulphur, which her imagination, stimulated by traditions of the ante-bellum aristocracy, had painted in very glowing colors ; but I told her it was impossible now, and so we kept our seats and went rushing southward again through the green hills that divide the headwaters of the Shenandoah from the tributaries of the James.

The Chesapeake and Ohio Railway, to which I have referred (or at least this part of it), was known before the war as the Virginia Central ; and as it was one of the two routes between Richmond and the Valley of Virginia, it was of great importance to the Confederates. To destroy it, therefore, became one of the objects of every Federal force in the valley, though that end was not achieved until Sheridan's successes of 1864.

Toward the close of that campaign the vicinity of Waynesboro became a continual skirmish-ground, and everything was laid waste. Before the winter of 1864–5 had passed, Sheridan again appeared in force, the cavalry sent to contest his advance proving inefficient. The Confederate commander, Jubal Early, had collected his army as well as he could and posted them upon a ridge just on the further (western) edge of Waynesboro, where Sheridan's advance came up with him on March 2d. "Custer at once sent three regiments around the enemy's left flank, while at the same time charging in front with the other two brigades. The position was carried in an instant, with

THE BLUE RIDGE, NEAR
WAYNESBORO.

little, if any loss on either side, and almost the entire force captured, all Early's wagons and subsistence, tents, ammunition, seventeen flags, eleven guns (including five found in the town) and, first and last, about 1,600 officers and men. . . . As for Early, Long, Wharton and the other Confederate generals, they fled into the woods, and Early himself soon after barely escaped capture by Sheridan's cavalry, while making his way to Richmond. The victory at Waynesboro left Sheridan complete master of the valley."

V.
CRAB-TREE FALLS AND THE NATURAL BRIDGE.

A Rougher Landscape.—Sources of the Shenandoah.—Crab-tree Falls.—Ascent of Three Thousand Feet of Cataracts.—View from Pinnacle Mountain.— Lexington and Loch Laird.—Approaching the Natural Bridge.— The Hotel.—Prue's Surprise.—Majesty of the Bridge.— The Attractions along Cedar Creek.—The Pic- ture from Above.—Surrounding Scenery and Amusements.—The Bridge by Moonlight.

THOUGH the vicinity of Waynesboro for some miles southward is a well cultivated farming and grazing region, by the time Stuart's Draft is reached the face of the country where the track passes has become too rough for farming, and the scene from the car windows is an ever-varying panorama of rugged hills and deep ravines. Almost the only signs of human occupation are small log-cabins, whose re-straint-hating, indolence-loving occupants earn a scanty-living by chopping logs ; gathering oak and hemlock bark (one of the leading products of this region, where large tanneries exist), and sumac leaves; in hunting, fishing and feeble farming. The hills we are passing across—a tangled series of folds belonging to the Blue Ridge—are called the Big Levees, and are dominated eastwardly by the Hump-back mountains. Their drainage forms the South River, and hence the uppermost source of the Shenandoah. The streams which go to make it up are countless, prattling down every green hollow. Now and then a pretty cascade is seen, like the Cypress falls opposite Riverside, leaping fierce and white out of the wooded precipice into a deep and quiet pool.

The greatest of all cataracts in the Virginia mountains, however, is the Crab-tree falls, reached by the old pike road from Vesuvius to Montebello and the Tye River valley east of the Blue Ridge. Sheridan once passed a large part of his army across the mountains by this road. At the very summit, from among the topmost crags of Pinnacle peak, one of the highest in Virginia, comes the Crab-tree to take its fearful course. Thence it descends three thousand feet in making a horizontal distance of two thousand, forming "a series of cascades athwart the face of the rock, over which the water shimmers in waves of beauty, like veils of lace trailed over glistening steel." The course of the stream is distinctly visible from a long distance down the face of the great crag, which contrasts sharply with the leafy masses on each side, and forms a striking landmark. The cascades vary from over five hundred feet in the highest to fifty or sixty in the lowest, and are greatly different in form and appearance. The Crab-tree is not a large stream ; in one or two places the entire body of water is com-pressed into a shooting jet not more than six inches in diameter, but, with the economy of nature, nothing is lost in artistic effect.

Three miles down Tye river the ascent of the falls is begun by entering the forest and a chaos of massive rocks. "The forest is so dense," says H. L. Bridgman, of New York, "that scarcely can the sunlight pierce it. Stately oaks, wide spreading maples and hickories, the birch and beech, with an occasional pine, and at rare intervals the light gray foliage of the cucumber-tree, make up a forest scene of wonderful beauty. Scarcely are we within the woods, when, looking aloft, we see through the leafy green of tree-tops the white spray of he 'Galvin' cataract, named in compliment to our guide, and 150 feet high. This is a clear, bold fall, and rather larger in volume and force than any of the others. The effects of the sunlight and shadow upon the fall and the forest are exceedingly graceful and picturesque, and from the beginning of the ascent all the way to the top the scene changes and shifts like a fairy panorama. . . . An hour or more of hard work and steady climbing brings us to the base of the 'Grand Cataract,' the first leap of the entire series, a clear fall of over 500 feet. It was the Grand Cataract which we had seen from the road far below, and looking upward from its base, the sight was like a sheet of foam falling out of a clear sky. The water, pure as crystal, is not projected with sufficient force to send it clear of the rock, and so it falls over its face, veiling the rugged front of the mountain as with a fleece. Standing at its base and looking upward, the spectator does not realize its immense height, but comparison of the lofty trees which tower into the heavens without approaching half the height of the falls demonstrates the fact. At the very top and crown of the fall, the configuration of the rock gives the current a sharp diagonal set which adds much to its picturesque beauty. Midway a ledge of a few feet wide arrests the fall and throws it boldly forward in a straight line again adown a sheer and glistening precipice of more than 200 feet. At the base of the Grand Cataract daisies bloom, and the waters are quite shallow."

It is possible to work one's way upward along these capricious cataracts to the very summit, and thence overlook a wide area of primitive mountain country. All about the observers tower peaks of the first rank, heaving against the blue of heaven a surging mass of foliage. "Dotting the mountain sides in every direction are cleared fields in which corn, wheat and tobacco are raised, the clearings sometimes extending to the very summits, while scattered here and there in all directions, nestling in the intervals and pockets of the ranges, are the log cabins of the moutaineers. Safe in these fortresses and upon a kindly and generous soil, with a genial and salubrious climate, the natives live from one generation to another an easy, thriftless and contented life. No one who sees the view from the head of the Crab-tree falls or Pinnacle mountain, no matter what his travels or experience in this or any other country have been or may be, will ever be able to forget its matchless charm, repose and serenity."

Through such a region as that we are now running, by the help of a thousand curves, deep cuttings or lofty bridges. Now and then

CRABTREE FALLS, VESUVIUS STATION, SHENANDOAH VALLEY R.R.

wonderful landscapes open out—far views southward and westward into the richly blue folds of the mountains, but chiefly our eyes are held by green dells, the romantic river, and the captivating bits of ruined canal, which arrange themselves for an instant close to the track only to dissolve into new pictures with kaleidoscopic speed.

Buena Vista is the appropriate name of a new and very progressive town founded within the past year upon the broad and nearly level plain between the mountains at this point. It forms one of the most interesting scenes along the route. The spectacle of this lovely valley, until recently only stirred from its silence by the shrill whistle of the passing locomotive, is an inspiring one. The enterprise is in the hands of the Buena Vista Company.

Upon a commanding plateau above the town stands a handsome hotel, reached by an excellent avenue. From this point of outlook is seen the many avenues of the town, graded away to the very bases of the hills, and along them numerous structures already completed, shops, stores and homes.

The large Buena Vista Iron Works occupies a central position, and an extensive tannery is also in operation. The excellent water-power of the picturesque North river is utilized by a paper mill, and many other industries are projected for the near future. At the point where the Shenandoah Valley and Chesapeake and Ohio tracks approach most closely, a handsome Union Depot has been completed. Schools and churches are already seen here and there, and every evidence of a substantial future is manifest to the visitor.

The primary cause of this remarkable growth is found in the presence of rich iron ore in large quantities in the immediate vicinity of the town. Ore openings may be found in almost any direction up among the hills, and no doubt narrow gauge railways will presently be built to the mines.

At Loch Laird, the next station, a town has been plotted and considerable progress made in development.

At Buena Vista we encounter the Chesapeake and Ohio Railway, which forms an exceedingly picturesque route from Richmond. Its only availability to us here would be as the means of access to Lexington, a town which southern people are fond of calling the " Athens of Virginia," because of its intellectual society and regard for books. This arises from the fact that since its foundation it has been a school town, and has now the celebrated Military Institute of which the most distinguished son was " Stonewall " Jackson, who is buried there.

" What river is this?" asks Prue, after we had been tracing the pretty stream for a few miles, having passed over the divide and now were beginning to follow descending instead of ascending currents.

" The South River," I reply.

" But I thought we had just left South River behind."

46

HOTEL BUENA VISTA, WEST VIEW.

"So we did. This is another, and a branch of the James. You might find a hundred South 'rivers,' 'forks,' 'branches,' and so on in the State. They were carelessly named by the people who never went—"

"Natural Bridge!" shouts the brakeman, and we hurriedly gather up our baggage and alight, with, perhaps, the most pleasurable anticipations of the whole trip.

It is two miles from the railway back into the broken hill country, where the Natural Bridge spans one of the mountain streams. Hacks from the hotel awaited the train, and our party had soon begun the drive. A short distance brought us out upon a sort of ledge, where, some hundreds of feet directly beneath us, we could see the noble James, deep, wide and glossy, forcing its way along in the dignity of fullness and strength. On the other side a great hill rose from the water, and as we attained higher and higher levels, other ridge-like summits appeared behind each more savage and lonely than the preceding.

The road is good and winds prettily among the hills, between a gulf on one side and tangled brush slopes on the other. It was with pleasing suddenness, too, that we emerged at last upon the broad lawns and parks of the hotel property, with its array of handsome dormitories, and its groups of smaller pleasure buildings, summer-houses and gardens. It was supper-time, and we were content for that night to sit on the veranda, listen to the ball-room music, breathe the cool, balsamic air, and sleep the sleep of weariness.

Breakfast was no sooner despatched next morning, however, than we hastened to satisfy our curiosity as to this great bridge "not built with hands," which justly ranks among America's "seven wonders."

The lawns are cleared around the head of a shallow ravine, the extreme upper point of which is occupied by an enormous mineral spring and fish basin. Down the ravine from the spring goes a well-graded pathway, which quickly disappears in the woods standing along the tumbling cascades of a brook that traverses the estate, and we follow it gleefully until it has descended three or four hundred feet into the leafy screen and rocky seclusion of one of Appalachie's most lovely glens. Prue has been sauntering on ahead, and turns a corner. As she does so we see her lift her head, a wide-eyed glow of surprise illumines her fair face, and she utters a little exclamation of delight. A step forward and we stand by her side and share her excitement—the bridge is before us!

The first impression is the lasting one—its majesty! It stands alone. There is nothing to distract the eye. The first point of view is at sufficient distance, and somewhat above the level of the foundation. Solid walls of rock and curtaining foliage guide the vision straight to the narrows where the archsprings colossal from side to side. Whatever questions may arise as to its origin, there is nothing hidden or mysterious in its appearance. The material of the walls is the material of the bridge. Its piers are braced against the mountains, its enormous keystone bears down with a weight which holds

BUENA VISTA SCENES

HOTEL BUENA VISTA, NORTH VIEW.

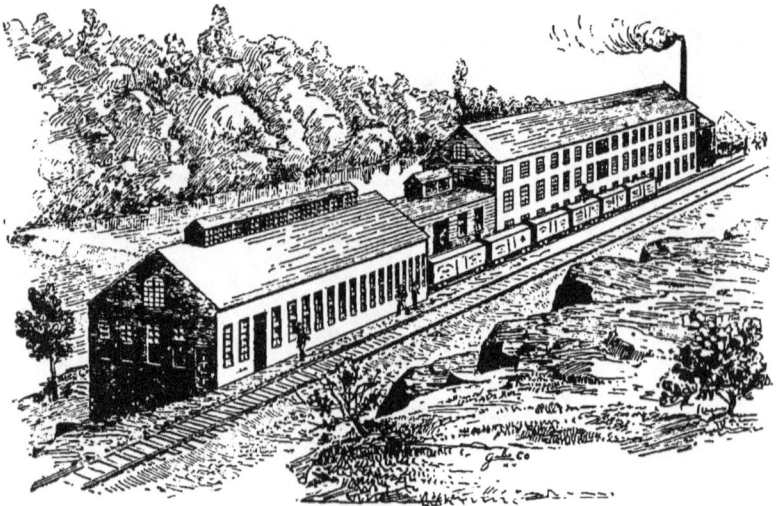

BUENA VISTA PAPER MILL.

GIANT ARBOR VITÆ, NATURAL BRIDGE RAVINE.

all the rest immovable, yet which does not *look* ponderous. Every part is exposed to our view at a glance, and all parts are so proportionate to one another and to their surroundings—so simple and comparable to the human structures with which we are familiar, that the effect upon our minds is not to stun, but to satisfy completely our sense of the beauty of curve and upright, grace and strength drawn upon a magnificent scale. " It is so massive," exclaims Mr. Charles Dudley Warner, "so high, so shapely, the abutments rise so solidly and spring into the noble arch with such grace and power! . . . Through the arch is the blue sky; over the top is the blue sky; great trees try in vain to reach up to it, bushes and vines drape and soften its outlines, but do not conceal its rugged massiveness. It is still in the ravine, save for the gentle flow of the stream, and the bridge seems as much an emblem of silence and eternity as the Pyramids."

Descending further the path cut along the base of the cliffs, which, as one writer has said, arise " with the decision of a wall, but without its uniformity—massive, broken, beautiful, and supplying a most admirable foreground." We advance under the arch, and gaze straight up at its under side which is from sixty to ninety feet wide. It is almost two hundred feet above the stony bed at Cedar creek, but Baily doesn't remember this, and fancies he can hurl a pebble to the ceiling. Vain youth! Even gentle Prue laughs at him, and the swallows weaving their airy flight in and out from sunlight to shadow, fearlessly swoop lower and twitter more loudly, deriding his foolish ambition.

Crossing the gay torrent on a foot-bridge, we wandered up the creek a mile or more, past Hemlock island; past the cave where saltpetre was procured for making powder, in 1812,

THE LOST RIVER.

and again during the Confederate struggle, and even penetrated the low portal within which a "lost" river murmurs and echoes to our

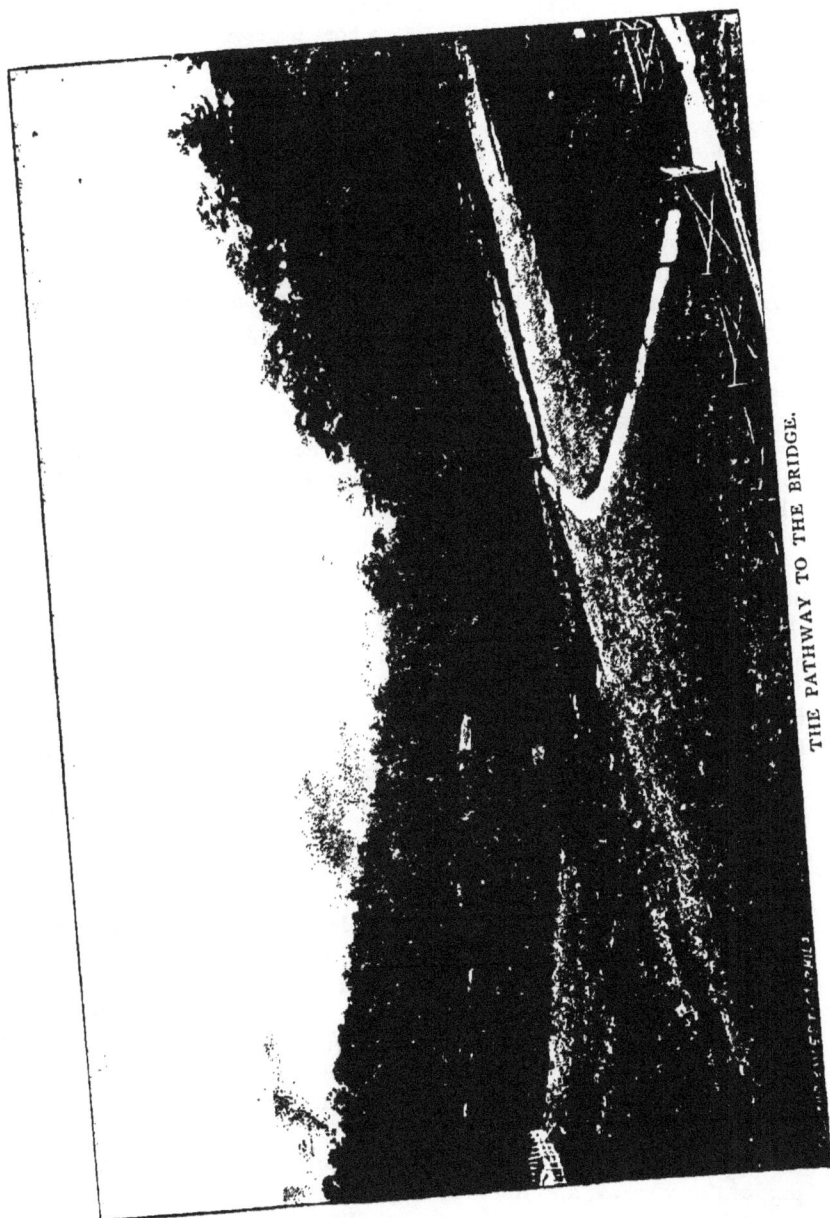

THE PATHWAY TO THE BRIDGE.

ears its unseen history, as it plunges through the dark recesses of its
subterranean course ; and the farther we went the more rugged,
thickly wooded and charmingly untamed was the gulch. Finally the
walls closed in altogether, but finding a boat we crossed to a stairway
of stone leading to Lace Water falls, where the stream leaps a hundred feet, falling in a dazzling *dishabille* of rainbow-tinted bubbles
and spray.

"The Glen" above the Bridge extends for a mile to Lace Water
Falls, where Cedar creek leaps one hundred feet from the upper
level. This glen was probably once an immense cave. The path
follows the stream or is cut into the rocks that form its bank. On the
right, a little above the Bridge, Cathedral Wall projects boldly,
covered with mosses and lichens. The precipice on the left is in color
light blue, and delicately traced with vines and evergreens. Farther
up, the cliffs on the right are red-brown, scarred and seamed, and
crowned with crags.

Hemlock island is an immense pyramid of evergreens.

The curious visitor is likely to step across the brawling little
stream along here, and peep into the gloom of a low-roofed cavern of
which more anon.

The upper part of the glen is densely wooded until the walls close
in and the path ends. A boat is here taken that lands at the Stone
Stairway. Climbing this, Lace Water falls are on the right. The
slopes and steps of the cascade are smooth, and the waters dash from
side to side fitfully, and weave a beautiful veil of foam and spray.

The Bridge seen from this (the upper) side is imposing, and its
magnitude is perhaps more striking ; but on the whole it is not so ef-
fective, regarded as an object by itself, as when studied from below.
Harriet Martineau, who once visited the spot, and has written enthu-
siastically of it in the second volume of her "Retrospect of Western
Travel" (1838), declares that she found most pleasure in looking at the
Bridge from the path just before reaching its base. "The irregular
arch," she writes, "is exquisitely tinted with every shade of gray and
brown , while trees encroach from the sides and overhang from the
top, between which and the arch there is an additional depth of fifty-
six feet. It was now early in July ; the trees were in their brightest
and thickest foilage ; and the tall beeches under the arch contrasted
their verdure with the gray rock, and received the gilding of the sun-
shine as it slanted into the ravine, glittering in the drips from the
arch, and in the splashing and tumbling waters of Cedar creek, which
ran by our feet."

Nevertheless, if you are willing to regard the great arch only as a
part of the *ensemble*, and to take into just account what is around and
beyond it as a proper part of the scene, I advise you to place yourself
a hundred yards *above* and then observe what a charming picture of
glistening torrent, flower-hung rocks, stately trees and far away
mountain crests is framed into its oval ; and how incomparable is the

VIEW OF THE NATURAL BRIDGE FROM BENEATH, LOOKING DOWN STREAM.

colossal frame itself—what sublimity of design—what wealth of dec-
oration and lavishness of color!

It cannot be too strongly insisted upon that while this curious
product of water erosion (slowing turning a cave into a long tunnel
and then, by the falling of the most of the roof, leaving only an arch-
like segment of the tunnel in the shape of a bridge) is the central at-
traction; there are a thousand other sources of enjoyment and pastime
at this pilgrimage-point.

For those who are content with rest and gossip, fresh air by day
and dancing at night, the fine new hotel offers every inducement for

TOP OF THE BRIDGE.

a prolonged stay. To the larger class which seeks more active pleasure during the summer vacation, a wide range of good roads and
interesting country is open for exploration. "The Bridge," says the
admirable little guide-book issued by the hotel people, "connects two
of five round-topped mountains that rise boldly from the great
valley of Virginia, near the confluence of James and North rivers,
These have been named Lebanon, Mars hill, Mount Jefferson, Lincoln
heights, and Cave mountain, and embraced in the park. Private
carriage-roads, nearly ten miles long, lead around or over them, and
give through arches cut in the forest, or from open spaces, a wonderful
variety and extent of mountain scenery.

" Eight hundred feet below the summit of Mt. Jefferson lie the green valleys of the rivers. Eight miles to the east the Blue Ridge forest-covered and mist-crowned, rises to its greatest height, 4 300 feet above the sea, and extends to north and south nearly one hundred miles before it is lost in the dim distance. A little to the left the glint of broken granite alone shows where the river bursts through, and at the right the crest lowers so that the Peaks of Otter may overlook. At the south, Purgatory mountain, and at the north, House mountain, throw their immense masses half across the plain. Against the western sky North mountain, the 'Endless mountain' of the Indians, lies cold and colorless. In the lifted central space of this great amphitheatre the park is located."

An old turnpike crosses upon the Bridge, but amid the apparently unbroken forest, few persons would discover it till told by the driver. In one of his inimitable articles in *Harper's Magazine*, before the war, Porte Crayon gives a ludicrous account of how his party behaved on the brink of the chasm ; and Miss Martineau confesses how her search was baffled. "While the stage rolled and jolted," she writes, "along the extremely bad road, Mr. L. and I went prying about the whole area of the wood, poking our horses' noses into every thicket and between any two pieces of rock, that we might be sure not to miss our object, the driver smiling after us whenever he could spare attention from his own not very easy task of getting his charge along. With all my attention I could see no precipice, and was concluding to follow the road without more vagaries, when Mr. L., who was a little in advance, waved his whip as he stood beside his horse, and said, 'Here is the Bridge !' I then perceived that we were nearly over it, the piled rocks on either hand forming a barrier which prevents a careless eye from perceiving the ravine which it spans. I turned to the side of the road, and rose in my stirrup to look over, but I found it would not do. . . . The only way was to go down and look up ; though where the bottom could be was past my imagining, the view from the top seeming to be of foliage below—foliage forever."

The bridle paths wind through in endless mazes.

Before crossing the Bridge the pedestrian will stop on Pulpit rock and Cedar cliff—wild, over-hanging crags, from which the Bridge and the glen are seen to advantage. After crossing, at the left a distant view of the valley is had from the dizzy height of Marshall's Pillar, and the path to the right, following along the edge of Rock Rimmond, leads to the Chimney's, Crow's Nest, the Black Gables, and Point Despair.

The driveways do not cease at the Bridge, but continue by an elevated course which gives some remarkable outlooks, and takes in various notable points.

The hotel is open all winter, and there are few days in this southern latitude when it would not be entirely comfortable to visit

THE SALTPETRE CAVE ON CEDAR CREEK.

all the points I have mentioned, and see the Bridge under a grimmer aspect, truly, than when mantled in the garlands of summer, yet with none of its grandeur diminished.

THE GRANT FROM GEORGE III.

To Thomas Jefferson in - - - - -	1774
To Joseph Lackland in - - - -	1833
To Houston & Cole in - - - - -	1838
To John B. Luster in - - - - -	1841
To Jesse Wooten in - - - - - -	1843
To John W. Garrett - - - - -	1849
To Anderson & Hitchcock in - - - -	1862
To Michael Harman in - - - - -	1863
To Asher Harman in - - - - -	1875
To H. C. Parsons in - - - - -	1881

HISTORICAL.—The earliest mention of the Bridge is by Burnaby, in 1759, who speaks of it as a "natural arch or bridge joining two high mountains with a considerable river underneath."

A bloody Indian fight occurred near here about 1770. Arrowheads, fragments of pottery, pipes, etc., are frequently found in the fields and roads of the neighborhood.

Lightning struck the bridge in 1779, and hurled down an immense mass of rock.

Washington when a surveyor for Lord Fairfax visited it, and carved his name where it may now be seen.

During the Revolution the French organized two expeditions to visit it. From their measurements and diagrams a picture was made in Paris, which for nearly half a century was copied in Europe and America as correct.

The place was much visited in the early part of this century. Marshall, Monroe, Clay, Benton, Jackson, Van Buren, Sam Houston, and others were registered here.

The original Bridge tract was granted by the king to Thomas Jefferson, in 1774. After he was president he visited the place, and surveyed and made the map with his own hands.

The next year he returned, bringing two slaves, Patrick Henry and wife. For them he built a log cabin with two rooms, and directed one to be kept open for the entertainment of strangers. The slaves were never manumitted and never recalled, the survivor dying where her master placed her twenty years before. Jefferson left here a large book "for sentiments." This was written full, and with its priceless record was accidentally destroyed, in 1845. Only a few extracts can be found. Jefferson spoke of it as yet to be "a famous place, that will draw the attention of the world." Marshall wrote of "God's greatest miracle in stone.", Clay, of "the bridge not made with hands, that spans a river, carries a highway and makes two mountains one."

Henry Piper, a student, in 1818, attempted to carve his name the highest, and found that he could not return. He then undertook the incredible feat of climbing to the top, and accomplished it.

Corbin Lackland fell from Pulpit Rock in 1833, and Robert Walker in 1845. Both were killed.

A stranger leaped from the Bridge in 1843, and his body was never identified.

John Rice fell from a crag, but was saved by the branches of a tree, in 1865.

Miss Randolph's celebrated adventure occurred on a large cedar stump, since demolished by relic hunters, which stood near the centre of the arch on the upper side.

The first hotel was built by Major Douthat, a Revolutionary soldier, in 1815, at a place about two miles north of the Bridge. An opposition hotel was built near the former in 1820. In 1828, Captain Lackland, also a Revolutionary soldier, built the first hotel on the location of the dwelling house of the present owner, calling it Jefferson Cottage. The Natural Bridge Hotel was built two years later.

At present the hotels consist of four principal buildings, Forest Inn, Appledore, Pavilion, and Bachelors' Lodge. These are supplied with running water and connected by bridges, and are in every respect elegantly furnished.

"Well," remarked Prue, when I had read over to her what I have written, "I *do* think you have made about as great a *failure* as I have ever seen. Why you haven't BEGUN to tell of *half* the good times we had at that *perfectly* LOVELY place !"

"I know it," I confess with humility.

"Well, *at least*," she went on, crushing my poor effort, "I would describe the gorge seen by *moonlight*. Don't you remember, Theo, that evening when we left the hop, stole away from the crowd on the piazzas and ran down the dewy lawn together?"

"You looked like a fairy that night, Prue, in your floating lace."

"And then, how we crept by those big, ogreish arbor-vitæ trees, and how you laughed at me, because I was a little timid in that dreadfully dark shadow under the crag ; and how we tried to hear words in the tinkle of rivulets down the ledges? Then, don't you remember with what a startle of delight we came in sight of the ravine, and you said the Bridge must have been carved out of silver and ebony? Can't you tell about that?"

"No, Prue—and I shouldn't like to try. Let those who come after us find it out for themselves as one of a hundred novel joys which await the sojourner at the Natural Bridge."

THE ARBOR-VITÆ TREES, AND GIANTS' STAIRWAY.

VI.

THE NEW CITY OF ROANOKE.

On the Bank of the James.—The Gap.—Buchanan's Iron Works.—A Town Saved by
its Captors.—Crossing to the Valley of the Roanoke.—Baily's Triumphant
Quotation.—Beginning and *raison d' etre* of Roanoke.—History
of the Consolidated Railways.—Amenities of Roanoke.—
Machine Works.—Iron Furnaces.—Stock
Yards.—Minor Factories.—The
Great Hotel.—Sunset
Pictures.

ROLLING slowly across the lofty iron bridge which carries the track
over the James at the Natural Bridge station, we skirt the base of the
mountains on the southern bank, and follow closely all the windings
of the stream. Not only is it impossible for the railway to leave its
margin, for the most part, but through long distances it has been
needful to dig into the foot of the precipitous hillside in order to make
room for the tracks. On the opposite side run the tracks of the Richmond and Alleghany Railroad, following the line of the disused canal,
whose broken dams still ruffle the current, and whose ruined locks are
sinking into shapeless decay.

As we approach Buchanan, the hills grow even steeper, and crowd
upon the river so closely that its current is greatly deepened and
confined, and rushes with noisy turbulence along a lane of gigantic
sycamores, willows and other water-loving trees, toward the gap
where the James bursts its way through the lofty cross-range of
Purgatory mountain. This gap is one which will especially interest
not only the scenery hunter, but the geologist; for, in the northern
wall of the gorge, where the river has exposed a vertical face of rock
of great height and breadth, it is easy to see how the rocks there
have been bent upward into an arch as high as the hill, the concentric
strata in which can be counted almost at a glance. Every exposed
cliff and railway-cutting gives evidence to the observant eye of how
the substance of these confused knolls and ridges has been con-
torted; but it is rare that so plain a cross-section of folding is offered
as in this exceedingly picturesque gap.

Between Waynesboro and Buchanan, the town which lies just
above the gap, many incidents of historical interest might have been
enumerated, and the names mentioned of many great men who were
its sons; but no consequential operations of either army in the late
war occurred there. At the latter town, however, began a series of
very memorable scenes.

On the evening of the 14th of June, 1864, Buchanan was noisy
with furnaces, forges, foundries and mills, especially the powerful
branch of Tredegar Iron Works, where cannon, ammunition, and
other iron supplies were cast for the Confederate government. Here
were flouring and blanket mills also, and in the neighborhood lay
farms producing food and forage for the army. In the town, as guard,
was McCausland with the cavalry which had just come back from

JAMES RIVER GORGE.

disasters before Sheridan. Demoralized and weak, these troopers were dismayed to hear that the Yankees were just across the river in great force, and would capture them all in a hurry. The river was easily fordable here, but McCausland (the same who set fire to Chambersburg and several Maryland villages), saw fit to burn the bridge against the protest of the citizens. From the burning bridge houses caught fire, and the whole town would have been destroyed had not the Yankee soldiers turned firemen and helped extinguish the

NEAR BUCHANAN

flames. This salvage accomplished, the captors (Hunter's fifteen thousand raiders) destroyed the ordnance factories which were so valuable to the Confederacy, and pushed toward the Peaks of Otter, "at a great expense of pioneer labor and bush fighting."

The James river, at Buchanan, passes close to its southern watershed; and having crossed the ridges which closely beset the town in that direction we are free from the grasp of the sterile and jungle-covered hills and descend into the valley of the Roanoke, through the farming and fruit raising districts of Houston, Troutville and Cloverdale. Seventy thousand apple trees were planted in Cloverdale alone during 1883; and—

"Cut it short!" Baily calls out with that disrespect for his elders which will be the death of him some day. "Here's our guide-book telling us all about it. Listen to this:

"We enter the Roanoke valley amid scenes of surpassing beauty. The setting sun purples the tops of the mountains and throws its slanting rays over the rich field and pasture lands; the twilight steals

out of the forest and dims the blue thread of mist along the James;
the cattle low in the shaded lanes, the sheep-bells tinkle on the hills;
Æolian winds ring among the dusky trees,

'Night draws her mantle and pins it with a star!'

"The city of Roanoke blazes up ahead like an illumination;
red-mouthed furnace-chimneys lift like giant torches above the plain;
the roar of machinery, the whistle of engines, the ceaseless hum of

CROZER IRON WORKS.

labor and of life in the very heart of a quiet mountain-locked valley.
We roll into the finest depot in the state, and are escorted to a hotel
that would do credit to the proudest city. We tourists go to bed
dumfounded!"

"That's the way to do it!" cries Baily, closing his book in triumph.
And that's just the way we did.

The nucleus of this city of Roanoke was a small village known as
the "Lick," where a salt lick, or saline impregnation of a piece of
marshy land, originally attracted the wild animals of the vicinity,
and, with the advance of settlement, the domestic animals of the
the pioneers. It was on a post-road, and had a tavern, store and
post-office, but is now simply a suburb tenanted wholly by negroes.

A MOUNTAIN RIFT, NEAR ROANOKE.

The country round about was exceptionally rich in agricultural land and forest growth, and soon attracted settlement and cultivation. On the opening of the Virginia and Tennesse Railway, in November, 1852, the business of the neighborhood naturally gravitated to the immediate vicinity of the line, and a town was started about the railway station called "Big Lick,"half a mile distant from "Old Lick," which finally became a hamlet of about 600 people.

In 1870, the Virginia and Tennessee, by consolidation with its connecting lines, became the Atlantic, Mississippi and Ohio Railroad, and this having become embarrassed in its finances was purchased by a syndicate of capitalists in Philadelphia, most of whom were already interested in the Shenandoah Valley Railroad, then in course of construction. It was decided to continue the latter line to a junction with the former at Big Lick (achieved in June, 1882), and operate them in association. The name of the Atlantic. Mississippi and Ohio Railroad was changed to Norfolk and Western. An operating arrangement for twenty-five years was concluded in September, 1881, with the East Tennessee, Virginia and Georgia Railroad, and its leased lines, and the Shenandoah Valley Railroad, and the entire system of 2,203 miles of railway has since that date been worked in entire harmony in all matters of general traffic, as the Virginia, Tennessee and Georgia Air Line. Economy and efficiency necessitated some central point for the control of the Norfolk and Western and Shenandoah Valley Railroads, the head-quarters of their direction, position of the shops for construction and repair of equipment, and residence of many of their employees. A company was therefore formed, which gradually bought several thousand acres of land around the junction, nearly all of which was farm land, procured the legal authority and laid out a town site, which was named Roanoke after the river which flows half a mile southward.

This was in the fall of 1881. Now Roanoke is a city of lively business appearance, and of new, modern, and in many cases very handsome houses, with a population of twenty thousand, and more coming. Its streets are lighted by gas, and the whole town is supplied with sweet, pure water drawn from "Big Spring" a mile and a half away, which is one of the most picturesque spots in the valley of the Roanoke river, whose lively current purls near by. The town contains a number of churches, good schools, a library association, an opera house, and various other means of mental and moral culture, as well as of material progress; while the presence of so many executive officers and their families, presupposes a society of more intelligence and social experience than is usually observed in so new a town.

"The requirements of such a population," says a recent report shown me by the indefatigable Baily, "almost entirely consumers, and the position of the city, at such an important railway junction, surrounded by an agricultural territory of such great productiveness,

GENERAL OFFICES OF THE SHENANDOAH VALLEY AND NORFOLK AND WESTERN RAILROADS AT ROANOKE.

with abundance of iron ores on every side, vast supplies of coal and coke within easy distance, and such a nucleus of manufacturing industry already established, seem to confirm the promise of a prosperity built upon the most solid foundation, and capable of indefinite expansion."

The largest element in the progress of Roanoke was the building of the Roanoke Machine Works, which owns a large tract of land and has constructed extensive buildings in the angle between the two roads. These buildings consist of brick shops, engine-houses and mills, for the construction of locomotives, stationary engines, cars of every grade and description, covering many thousands of square feet, and are supplied with all the ponderous and complicated machinery necessary to make all sorts of bridges, and all kinds of cast or forged iron work. This does not mean merely that the machinery or cars may be put together here ; but, except a few specialties, every part of the locomotive or car, from the wheels to the last ornament, is made and fitted as well as "set up" here. It would be out of place in a pamphlet of this nature to give an extended description of such works, to which these railways look for nearly all their rolling stock ; but the visitor to

BIG SPRING, NEAR ROANOKE.

Roanoke will find it well worth his while to go through them.

The raw material of iron and steel used is largely supplied by the Crozer Steel and Iron Company, whose blast-furnace is a quarter of a mile away, and another object of interest to tourists, who often go at night to witness the thrilling spectacle of drawing the molten iron from the furnace into the molds where it will be cast in "pigs." This company derives its ores (brown hematite) mainly from the upland mines owned by it near Blue Ridge station, ten miles eastward, and from the Houston mines, fifteen miles northward. The yield sometimes reaches a hundred tons a day, and the greater part is marketed in Pennsylvania in successful competition with local manufacturers. Another similar enterprise is the Rohrer Iron Company, which owns extensive deposits of high grade limonite ore, half a dozen miles south of town. This property is reached by a narrow gauge railway, which may ultimately be extended through to

HOTEL ROANOKE.

the Danville and New River Railroad, in North Carolina, and at its terminus in West Roanoke the company owns land upon which it now stores and ships its products, and will probably construct a furnace. Near there are the Roanoke stock-yards, where abundant conveniences for the transference of cattle are provided, together with a hotel for the drovers and traders, having telegraphic communication with northern markets.

In addition to these larger concerns many smaller ones contribute to the prosperity of the place; such as tobacco factories, lumber-working mills, cigar-making shops, spoke factories, bottling works, and the like. So rapid and persistent has been the growth of the little city, the site of which three years ago was all a wheat field, that although the Town Company had expended $600,000, its profits have been very satisfactory.

For the equestrian, the vicinity of Roanoke is full of opportunities. A hard, even road leads away eastward over the ridge, where most of the handsome homes of the residents are built, and brings us to the Big Spring, a fountain-head of water sufficiently powerful to run the huge wheel of a flour-mill, and to supply the city with a plentitude of the purest water.

To the westward other roads wind away into the hills. Under the pilotage of two genial citizens we made a saddle journey of discovery in this direction. We found, hidden away

TINKER AND MILL MOUNTAINS, ROANOKE.

in the peaceful seclusion of a pretty valley, the Hollins Institute, a popular seminary for young ladies, always filled with merry and bright-eyed maidens from every state of the South, under tuition of an excellent corps of instructors. Two miles beyond we came upon one of those sermons in stone which are as an open page to the geologist—a rift in the ledge

1.—A SHADY PORCH.   HOTEL ROANOKE.   2.—MAIN STAIRWAY.

where a little fretful stream poured down between the rocky jaws
over the ruins of a log dam and past the remnants of a flume and
mill—as pretty a bit of rockscape as one will find in these mountains.
Here the pent-up waters of a vast inland lake have sometime burst
through and scattered the fragments of the massive gateway right
and left through the valley. We found just time to make a hasty
sketch, and retraced our steps to the Institute, beneath the hospitable
roof of which we tarried that night.

Returning to Roanoke in the morning by the mountain road, our
artist halted to add the bold outlines of Tinker and Mill mountains to

his sketch-book, and we wished, when we drew rein at the hotel an
hour later, that our ride had been twice as long.

The three buildings which catch the eye of the traveler, and
surprise him are the railway station and its "low-ceiled, dainty"
eating-house in the Queen Anne style—though as Charles Dudley
Warner said of it, that queen probably never sat in so tasteful a
a dining-room or had so good a dinner; the railway head-quarters,
falling in a cataract of peaked roofs and balconied fronts down the
slope of the street; and the splendid hotel crowning the hill in the
midst of lawns, parterres of flowers and ceaseless fountains. In the

LOBBY OF THE HOTEL ROANOKE.

presence of the accompanying illustrations it would be superfluous to
describe their outward appearance.

Interiorly—to speak now of the Hotel Roanoke—the wood-work
is hard pine, finished in the natural grain; the furniture ash and
cherry, and all the arrangements tasteful as well commodious. The
parlor is as pretty a room as you will find in many a mile, and the
dining-room light and cheerful, with small tables and growing
plants. The table and service are of a high order; and I do
not know a better resting place for the tourist than this. All this may
seem high praise for a hotel, but it is given ungrudgingly. We spent
a good many pleasant days there and paid for them squarely; hence
I can say what I please, and sum it up in the candid opinion that
Hotel Roanoke has nothing to approach it (save at Luray) between
Philadelphia and Florida.

There was a certain corner of one of the upper piazzas a little out
of the way, where we used to like to sit an hour or so after tea,

smoking our evening cigars, watching the glories of the sunset, and discussing things in a hopeful strain that would have vexed Michiavelli to the soul. The mountains stand in an irregular circle about Roanoke, none too near for the best effect, and the western view is an especially fine one. The lowering orb of light sinks grandly behind the line of mountain wall, across whose serrations its last rays gush in a blinding effulgence which slowly pales away through every rosy and nacreous tint into the sweet twilight of the summer night. I remember a remark by Prue, that the day here was like the fabled dolphin which in its death put on a shimmering robe of swiftly changing colors, and so passed away gloriously. Nor is the beauty all in the sky, for the foreground is, nearest, the picturesque structures of the town, then a billowy stretch of green and bosky knolls, and finally the obliquely retreating array of the Alleghanies, where

> " headland after headland flame
> Far into the rich heart of the West."

THE ROANOKE.

The Luray Cave and Hotel Company.

NOTICE TO VISITORS.

To prevent confusion or misunderstanding, and to guard against imposition, visitors are requested to pay particular attention to the following regulations :—

ADMISSION TO THE CAVERNS.

Visitors are admitted to the Caverns from 7.00 a.m. to 6.00 p.m., during which time no charge is made for the electric light. After 6.00 p.m. a special charge is made for admission, and the electric light will not run unless by special arrangement.

From 7.00 a.m. till 6.00 p.m., including electric light, - -	*$1.00*
After 6.00 p.m., without electric light, - - - -	*1.50*

A special charge will be made as follows for electric light, if desired by visitors after 6.00 p.m.:—

In Addition to the Night Rate of Admission.

For ONE Visitor, - - - - - - -	*$2.00*
" TWO Visitors, (each), - - - - - -	*1.00*
" THREE " " - - - - - -	*75*
" FOUR " " - - - - - -	*50*
" FIVE " " - - - - - -	*25*

For SIX or MORE Visitors, NO EXTRA CHARGE will be made.

N. B.—A small charge is made at the Cave House for taking care of articles of baggage.

Cave Photographs, Specimens, Guide Books, etc., may be purchased at fixed prices. No other charges than those specified are permitted.

Ordinary clothing should be worn in the Caverns. Ladies should wear overshoes. No special changes of dress are needed, and extra wraps are superfluous—the cave temperature being 56° F. at all seasons. Canes, sticks, etc., are not allowed in the Caverns. Smoking is prohibited.

☞ Visitors are urgently requested to aid in protecting the formations in the Caverns from defacement and mutilation.

☞ Under the laws of Virginia, persons detected in breaking or defacing the formations may be arrested and fined.

CAVE HACKS.

Authorized Hacks make regular trips to the Caverns. Special trips will be made from the Railroad Station and from the Inn when required. Railroad coupons for hack transportation will be honored on any trip of authorized hacks.

Rates per Round Trip.

Per Passenger on REGULAR trips from Railroad Station, - *35 Cents.*
Per Passenger on SPECIAL trips from the Inn or Railroad Station, 50 Cents.

N.B.—Visitors are particularly requested to retain the "RETURN" hack coupon until they return from the Caverns, and not to surrender it on the "GOING" trip to the Caverns.

CAVERNS OF LURAY,

LURAY STATION,	**E. J. ARMSTRONG,**
Shenandoah Valley R.R.	Superintendent.

List of Agents of the Shenandoah Valley Route.

FOR THROUGH TICKETS, TIME TABLES, SLEEPING CAR RESERVATIONS, TOURISTS'
GUIDE BOOKS AND GENERAL INFORMATION,
Apply to or address by mail any of the following Offices

IN THE NORTH AND EAST:

BOSTON, No. 3 Old State House; 205, 211, 214, 232, 290 and 322 Washington St.; and at the Depots of the New York Lines; C. P. GAITHER, New England Agent, 290 Washington St.; J. H. MCCORMACK, Traveling Agent.

Also at Railroad Ticket Offices at Providence, Worcester, Springfield, Hartford, New Haven, Bridgeport, Stamford, etc.

NEW YORK, at No. 1 Astor House; No. 8 Battery Place; 415, 435, 849 and 944 Broadway; 134 East 125th St.; Depots foot of Desbrosses and Courtlandt Sts., and Office of Line, 303 Broadway. L. J. ELLIS, General Eastern Passenger Agent; JAMES E. PRINDLE, New York Passenger Agent. Telephone number, John 563.

BROOKLYN, at No. 4 Court St., and Office of Brooklyn Annex, foot Fulton St.

JERSEY CITY, at Penn. R. R. Depot Ticket Office; also at Passenger Station Ticket Offices Penn. R. R., at Elizabeth, Rahway, New Brunswick and Trenton, N. J.; Newark, 789 Broad St. and Market St. Station.

PHILADELPHIA, at Nos. 838, 833 and 1348 Chestnut St., and Broad St. Depot; also at R. R. Ticket Offices Penn. R. R. at Germantown, Pa.; Chester, Pa.; Wilmington, Del.

HARRISBURG, at Ticket Office of Cumberland Valley R. R.; also Ticket Offices Northern Central R. R., Williamsport, Elmira, Canandaigua, etc.

BUFFALO, 19 Exchange St. and 11 East Main St., Rochester, N. Y.

PITTSBURGH, at Penn. Railroad Ticket Office.

BALTIMORE, at Ticket Offices B. & P. and B. & O., Western Maryland R. R., 217 East Baltimore St., at Depot Western Maryland R. R., and Office of Line, 129 East Baltimore St. KENNON JONES, Agent.

WASHINGTON, at B. & O. Offices. M. DU PEROW, Pass. Agent, 1433 Penn'a Ave.

HAGERSTOWN, MD., at Depot Shenandoah Valley Railroad. C. M. FUTTERER, Passenger Agent.

IN THE SOUTH AND SOUTHWEST AT

NEW ORLEANS, Ticket Offices and Depots L. & N. R. R., and Great Jackson Route and Queen and Crescent Route, and Mississippi Valley Route. J. C. ANDREWS, Gen'l Southern Agent. JAS. H. HILL, Ticket Agent, 22 Carondelet St.

MOBILE, Ticket Office, opposite Battle House, and Depot Ticket Offices L. & N. R. R., and M. & O. R. W. H. DOLL, T. P. A., M. & B. Ry.

SELMA, C. T. AIRBY, Ticket Agent; L. A. BELL, A. G. P. A.

MONTGOMERY, Depot Ticket Office Western R. R. (of Ala.), and L. & N. R. R. JNO. M. WYLY, General Agent; W. F. ALLDAY, Traveling Passenger Agent.

JACKSONVILLE, Ticket Office S., F. & W. R'y. FRANK M. JOLLY, District Passenger Agent, 75 Bay Street.

ST. AUGUSTINE, F. J. BALLARD, Ticket Agent. S., F. & W. R'y.

MACON, A. B. QUINKER, Ticket Agent, Depot E. T., V. & G. R'y, and Ticket Office, 100 Second Street.

MERIDIAN, MISS., J. D. WADDELL, Agent.

ROME, GA., C. P. KENNEDY, City Passenger and Ticket Agent, Armstrong Hotel.

ATLANTA, Ticket Office E. T., V. & G. R'y Depot, and Ticket Office, No. 1 Kimball House. T. C. STURGIS, Traveling Passenger Agent; C. N. KIGHT, Assistant Gen'l Passenger Agent.

RICHMOND, VA., Ticket Offices at A. W. GARBER's, 1000 Main St., and Depot of C. & O. R'y.

NORFOLK, Ticket Offices, W. T. WALKE, Atlantic Hotel and Depot N. & W. R. R. F. H. MASI. Masi's Drug Store; H. W. JAMES, Agent, Norfolk.

DALLAS, TEX., Depot Ticket Office Texas Pacific R. R. and H. & T. C. R y.

LITTLE ROCK, ARK., Depot Ticket Office M. & L. R. R. R. C. A. BAIRD, Gen'l Western Passenger Agent.

MEMPHIS, TENN., Depot Ticket Office M. & C. R. R. BARNEY HUGHES, Ticket Agent, 278 Main St.; J. C. BEAM, City Passenger Agent; C. A. DESAUSSURE, Assistant General Passenger Agent.

NASHVILLE, TENN., Depot Ticket Office N. C. & St. L. R'y, and Robertson's Ticket Office, Maxwell House.

CHATTANOOGA, Ticket Office Union Passenger Depot. J. M. SUTTON, District Passenger Agent.

CLEVELAND, TENN., J. M. CROW, Passenger Agent.

ATHENS, TENN., D. M. OWEN, Passenger Agent.

SWEETWATER, TENN., A. W. LILLARD, Passenger Agent.

KNOXVILLE, Ticket Office E. T., V. & G. R'y. J. L. MILAM, Passenger Agent; W. A. DAY, District Passenger Agent, Asheville, N. C.

LYNCHBURG, WARREN L. ROHR, Passenger and Ticket Agent. Ticket Office Depot Norfolk & Western R. R. J. L. PECK, Commercial Agent.

ROANOKE, J. B. PACK, Ticket Agent; ALLEN HULL, Traveling Passenger Agent.

And at all Principal Railroad Ticket Offices Throughout the Country.

TABLE OF STATIONS, DISTANCES, Etc.

Station No.	STATIONS.	County and State.	Miles from Hagerstown.	Feet above Tide.
0	Hagerstown	Washington, Md.	....	566
6	St. James	" "	5.9	467
9	Grimes	" "	9.0	382
14	Antietam	" "	14.1	445
17	Sheperdstown	Jefferson, W. Va.	16.9	405
23	Shenandoah Junction	" "	23.1	515
28	Charlestown	" "	29.4	517
33	Ripon	" "	33.7	519
36	Gaylord	Clarke, Va.	36 2	522
40	Berryville	" "	39.9	571
46	Boyce	" "	46.2	575
49	White Post	" "	49.2	610
53	Ashby	Warren, "	53.2	600
56	Cedarville	" "	56.4	589
59	Riverton	" "	59.2	497
62	Front Royal	" "	62.1	495
66	Manor	" "	66.4	497
73	Bentonville	" "	72.9	732
76	Overall	Page, "	75.6	662
80	Rileyville	" "	79.8	726
85	Kimball	" "	85.1	895
89	LURAY	" "	88.8	822
96	Marksville	" "	95 6	1,066
102	Ingham	" "	101.8	946
104	Grove Hill	" "	104.0	966
107	Milnes	" "	106.7	940
113	Elkton	Rockingham, "	112.5	958
127	Port Republic	" "	127.2	1,096
129	GROTTOES	Augusta, "	129.1	1,128
132	Harriston	" "	132.1	1,135
137	Crimora	" "	136.9	1,242
143	Waynesboro Junction	" "	143.2	1,293
148	Lyndhurst	" "	149.0	1,330
150	Lipscomb	" "	150.0	1,380
153	Stuart's Draft	" "	153.0	1,386
160	Greenville	" "	159.4	1,548
163	Lofton	" "	162.7	1,785
168	Vesuvius	Rockbridge, "	167.6	1,420
175	Midvale	" "	174.9	1,084
180	Riverside	" "	179 7	938
186	Loch Laird	" "	185 9	812
189	Thompson	" "	188 7	790
191	Buffalo Forge	" "	191.0	756
199	NATURAL BRIDGE	" "	198 6	760
209	Arcadia	Botetourt, "	208.9	796
214	Buchanan	" "	214.2	871
219	Lithia	" "	219.2	970
225	Houston	" "	224.6	1,348
228	Troutville	" "	227.9	1,306
232	Cloverdale	" "	232.2	1,125
236	Tinker Creek	Roanoke, "	236.5	966
239	Roanoke	" "	239.3	907

ONLY ALL-RAIL ROUTE

— TO THE —

Wonderful Caverns of Luray,

THE FAMOUS

Natural Bridge of Virginia,

AND THE

Grottoes of the Shenandoah.

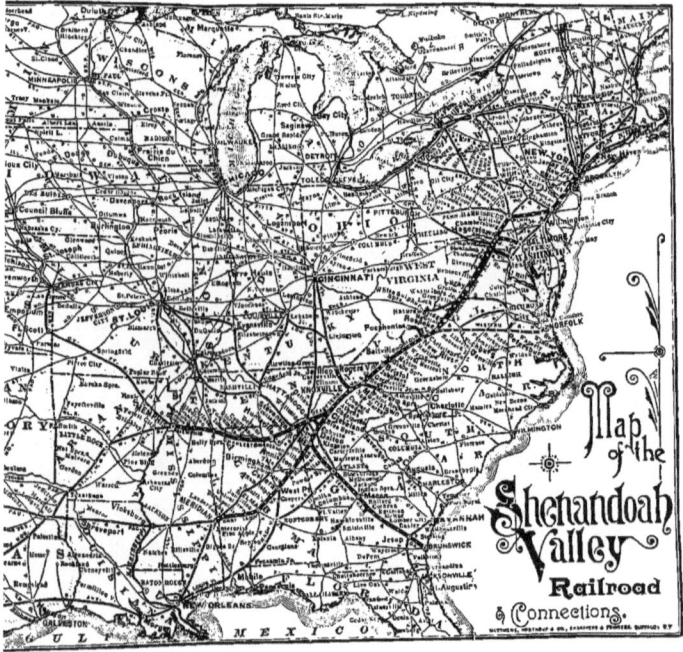

Map of the Shenandoah Valley Railroad & Connections.